How to Grow
ROSES

By the Editors of Sunset Books and Sunset Magazine

LANE BOOKS • MENLO PARK, CALIFORNIA

ACKNOWLEDGMENTS

Since the beginnings of recorded history, men have been writing about roses. It is, therefore, no small undertaking to distill so many centuries of rose lore into one book. Take almost any aspect of the rose—history, culture, the roses themselves—and an entire volume could be devoted to it. Fortunately, experienced rosarians are not only knowledgeable but also have been very generous with their time in helping us select and evaluate basic information which would benefit the novice rose grower and tomorrow's dyed-in-the-wool rose enthusiast.

For their invaluable aid in preparing this book we would like to thank Dr. R. C. Allen, Mansfield, Ohio; David H. Berg, Bloomfield, Connecticut; Edwin A. Birge, Carrollton, Georgia; Charles P. Dawson, Finchville, Kentucky; Fred Edmunds, Wilsonville, Oregon; George Haight, San Jose, California; Mrs. Muriel Humenick, Sunnyvale, California; Rudy Kalmbach, Portland, Oregon; Frank J. Lacoma, Omaha, Nebraska; Ross V. Lahr, Littleton, Colorado; Dr. C. A. Rohrer, Winona, Minnesota; Carson Scoggins, Shreveport, Louisiana; Mrs. Dorothy Stemler, Watsonville, California; John van Barneveld, La Habra, California; and Howard Walters, Houston, Texas.

Also, we extend a very special thanks to two past presidents of the American Rose Society—Mrs. Helene Schoen, Vancouver, Washington; and Joseph Klima, Kentfield, California.

Color photographs on pages 34 through 62 taken especially for this book are, with few exceptions, the work of Ells Marugg who is to be commended for his patience, perseverance, good humor, and readiness always to go on to another garden in search of the elusive "perfect blossom."

COVER: *'Sunset Jubilee'*

Commemorating the 75th Anniversary of the founding
of *Sunset* Magazine is this new hybrid tea rose 'Sunset Jubilee,'
whose pink and cream tones mirror the beauty of a late afternoon Western sky. Photograph by Glenn Christiansen.

Edited by Philip Edinger

Design: John Flack

Illustrations: Vernon Koski

Executive Editor, Sunset Books: David E. Clark

Third Printing January 1974

CONTENTS

Special Features

FIRST INTRODUCED by France's Empress Josephine, the large public rose garden has flourished as a convenient place to view new varieties as well as established favorites—well cared for in attractive settings.

Introducing the Queen

WHEN you invite the rose to grace your garden, you welcome not only a plant that provides great beauty but also one that proudly carries a rich heritage of legend and history. Sacred flower of Aphrodite and Venus, inhabitant of Eden, its blossoms perfuming ancient Babylonian and Persian gardens, the rose has been a special flower to all cultures that have known it.

Just one look at the modern rose will illustrate why it has been repeatedly called the "queen of flowers." And yet it was the Greek poetess Sappho who bestowed this title on the rose—in 600 B.C., when roses were far removed from their modern refinement. Obviously there was "something" even then about the simple roses that caused them to stand out from their fellow flowers in a regal and femininely beautiful way. Roses did not escape the notice of another literary Greek: Homer referred to them in both his epics, the *Odyssey* and the *Iliad*. And in a strictly formal reference, the natural scientist Theophrastus wrote a botanical account of roses in the 4th century B.C.

Although the Greeks may have been the first to have had a word for it, earlier civilizations held the rose in equally high regard but chose to demonstrate their affection through other art forms. Asian coins minted as long ago as 4,000 B.C. are adorned with the rose motif. Frescoes dating from 1,600 B.C. uncovered on the Mediterranean island of Crete distinctly portray blossoms of single roses. Of similar antiquity are architectural decorations fashioned after roses found in ruins of the Assyrian and Babylonian civilizations that once flourished in present-day Iraq.

While all these ancient cultures glorified and stylized the rose, it remained for the Romans to bring it down to earth: they loved roses in a very physical sense. Hardly a public or private ceremony took place without roses playing a part. Blossoms were used at weddings, funerals, in conferring military honors, as party decorations (for the room *and* the guests), in perfumery, and for medicinal purposes. A wealthy Roman could be bathed in rose water, drink rose wine, eat confections made from roses, and party in rooms strewn with their petals. Because of such widespread use, commercial rose growing became a profitable Roman industry. Aside from Rome itself, Egypt was the principal supplier, although all Roman colonies grew roses to supply the needs of their officials.

The decorative use of roses reached a frenzy during the infamous rule of their emperor Nero. Rose petals at one festive gathering, for example, were so deep that a number of the guests suffocated in them—helped along, probably, by too much rose wine. On the scholarly side, Pliny, in his *Natural History*, recorded valuable information concerning the identification of the different types, colors, and growth habits of the roses then in cultivation.

ROSES SINCE ROME

Since they were identified so closely with Roman excesses, it is no wonder that roses fell out of favor with the early Christian church. Fortunately, this stigma was cast aside rather quickly, and the rose became the symbol, instead, for survivors of religious persecution, the white rose representing the Virgin Mary. Of all its religious representations, the most magnificent expression probably is the "rose window"—a standard component of medieval cathedrals. Intricately fashioned from stained glass, these huge translucent panels are circular in design with "petals" radiating from the window's center.

From the earliest days of chivalry, the rose was a favored motif for heraldic crests and a design element in the banners and shields of numerous European noblemen. Several English monarchs—beginning with Edward I in 1272—adopted the rose as their badge. Roses were made tragically famous in the conflict between the English houses of York and Lancaster, whose emblems were, respectively, a white and a red rose. Legend has it that the red-and-white striped rose known as 'York and Lancaster' appeared soon after conclusion of the War of the Roses in 1485.

Interest in roses during the thousand or so years between the fall of the western Roman empire and the Renaissance in Europe was kept alive largely in the hundreds of Christian monasteries scattered throughout western Europe. Not only were roses important symbolically to the religion, but also they had a number of medicinal uses ascribed to them, and it was in monasteries that most medieval knowledge was kept alive. Roses were cultivated there in medicinal herb gardens.

Although Romans cultivated a number of different roses from those growing in their empire and later Christians perpetuated these sorts in cloistered gardens, credit for initial discovery and spread of exotic species must go to the Moslem Arabs. Not long after the fall of Rome, they began extending their holdings from the Near East into western Europe on one hand and into the far East on the other. In Persia, India, and China, they encountered entirely different roses which they carried westward, just as they took western species to the East. Unfortunately, many of these died out after the Moslems were driven from their European landholdings and would have to wait 200-400 years for re-introduction to European gardens.

The Emperor's New Roses

From the viewpoint of modern rose culture, nothing is historically so important as the enthusiasm for roses generated by the Empress Josephine, wife of France's Napoleon I. At her disposal she had almost unlimited funds, manpower, and influence, enabling her to collect and maintain nearly all species and hybrids known at that time. Begun in 1804, the rose collection at the imperial château Malmaison was complete ten years later—with around 250 different roses represented. The fame of Josephine's rose garden was international, and so great was respect for it that even the British—then at war with France—permitted plants found on captured French ships to be sent on to Malmaison. At the end of hostilities in 1815, occupying British troops were ordered to protect the garden from harm.

The Empress also summoned a group of artists to her rose garden so that the forms and colors of her collected roses might be preserved for posterity. Among these artists was Pierre-Joseph Redouté—the "Raphael of the flowers"—whose water-color paintings of Josephine's roses later were published in a three-volume work, *Les Roses*, accompanied with botanical descriptions by Thory. Even at the time the descriptions were bettered in earlier publications, but to this day the work remains unsurpassed by the beauty and detail of Redouté's illustrations.

A glance at the most prominent types of roses in Josephine's garden will give an idea of what was grown popularly up to that time and also a look at the ancestors of modern roses.

More than half of her 250-odd roses were what are called "Gallicas"—varieties, and in some cases hybrids, of *Rosa gallica*. Known also as the French rose, the species grows wild in many parts of Western Europe and western Asia and has escaped cultivation to "go native" in some areas of North America. The color range

CHEROKEE ROSE (Rosa laevigata) *typifies wild roses: single, 5-petalled. Common in the South, it is a Chinese native.*

extends from rich maroon and dark red shades through pink to white and a number of striped combinations. Typically, the Gallicas are very hardy, adaptable, and vigorous; in addition, the species is quite variable, and most of its varieties have a strong tendency to produce mutations and to hybridize freely with other roses. Little wonder that they were the most popular group of garden roses up to the time of Malmaison. Their chief drawback is that they flower only once each year.

About one-eighth of the Malmaison collection consisted of *Rosa centifolia* varieties and hybrids—the centifolias or "cabbage roses" having up to 100 petals packed into each flower. The fullness of their blossoms was distinctive and unique; it was a disadvantage, however, in that very often the flowers could not open completely—the buds would "ball" before unfolding to expose the flower's center. Colors included white and all shades of pink but none of the rich reds found in the Gallicas; and cabbage roses, too, have only one flowering season. Their chief claim to fame is the moss rose, the first of which appeared around 1700 as a mutation on *Rosa centifolia*. To the charm of a full-petalled flower, the moss roses added a dense covering of mossy glands on the unopened buds, flower stems, and sometimes even of leaflets.

Of the somewhat mysterious Damask roses, Josephine had only nine. There was no mystery as to what they were, but there is great uncertainty about their origin and—most importantly—how some of them acquired the ability to flower more than once yearly. In the western world, *Rosa damascena* made its first documented appearance in ancient Egypt, but not as a native plant. Although its name is taken from Damascus, Syria, the species seems to have come west from Asia, brought by Phoenician traders or Greek colonials, if not by the Egyptians. The Romans knew it as the "Rose of Paestum" (or of Cyrinae or Carthage), and its likeness appears on frescoes in Pompeii. Much later, Spanish missionaries brought it to North America, where it is known as the "Rose of Castile." The damask fragrance is legendary; even today acres of a form called 'Kazanlik' are grown to produce the petals from which the fragrance "attar of roses" is extracted. Until the Oriental roses made their European debut late in the 1700s, the autumn damasks were the only roses to repeat bloom, however modestly, during the year.

At the same time that the awareness of roses was being fostered by Josephine, the British, French, and Dutch were making important horticultural discoveries in the Orient—a part of the world quite out of contact with western Europe until the 17th and 18th centuries. The East India Companies of these three countries established posts in China and India where, among many fascinating new plants, were roses quite different from those familiar in Europe. These were collected and sent back to individuals and botanic gardens in nothern Europe, from which they often were distributed as quickly as new plants could be propagated.

'AUSTRIAN COPPER' is gold and flame color form of Rosa foetida, *source of yellow and orange shades in modern roses.*

Because her collection contained the *avant garde* roses as well as the *déja vu*, Josephine grew as many of the "Chinas" as she could get: about 22. The first of these Oriental roses to reach western Europe arrived in the 1780s, their popularity assured because they honestly came close to being everblooming. Two forms were brought in at the same time: the pink 'Old Blush' and 'Old Crimson China.' Both presumably are just varieties of *Rosa chinensis* but represented centuries of selection for better flowered forms by Chinese horticulturists, who began with the single-flowered species and gradually developed forms with many petals. Overwhelmingly in their favor was their frequency of bloom; their liability was tenderness to cold and, compared with Damasks and Gallicas, their slight fragrance.

The Malmaison collection contained other rose species and natural hybrids, but with these four types, the family group was assembled which would, in the span of less than 100 years, revolutionize the rose.

19th Century Development

Until the time of Josephine and for several decades afterward, the development of new roses was entirely in the hands of Mother Nature. Now and then, a mutation would occur on an established sort. But by far the most common means of obtaining new roses was by planting seeds. The species and their varieties contained enough inherent variability so that it was not uncommon for seedlings to differ (slightly to considerably) in appearance from their seed parent. If two different roses grew side by side (a Gallica next to a Damask, for example), it was always possible that some of the seeds taken from either one might have resulted from the pollen of the other—a truly hybrid cross.

With the influx of new roses from the Orient, distinctly different roses began cropping up in seedling plantings: hybrids between European and Chinese or Indian sorts. The new combinations found in these seedlings fired the imaginations of horticulturists, botanists, nurserymen, and gardeners alike. More and more seeds were sown annually, resulting in rapid development of several new types of roses during the 19th century—and culminating in the first hybrid teas which have come to dominate 20th century rose gardens.

Portland Roses were the first new group to emerge, around 1800. Although their ancestries vary, all apparently were derived from the Autumn Damasks. Sometimes catalogued as Damask Perpetuals, they were almost always called Portland Roses after their first representative, 'Duchess of Portland.' To roses that offered some, if slight, hope of repeat bloom, the best of them brought the rich Gallica red and increased doubleness from Centifolias. For about fifty years they maintained some popularity until they were eclipsed by their own descendants, the hybrid perpetuals (see this page).

Hybrid China roses include a diverse group of plants whose characteristics are hard to generalize. Some rebloom, others don't—depending upon the other parent. Those derived from 'Old Blush' had white or pink flowers, whereas hybrids of 'Old Crimson China' generally retained its red color. Where the closely related species, *Rosa odorata* entered into a hybrid's background, it is difficult to place the plant as a hybrid China or tea rose (see this page). Ironically, the important old Bourbon—China hybrid 'Gloire des Rosomanes,' which is one of the primary sources of red color in today's hybrid teas, has persisted in countless gardens today but under the name 'Ragged Robin'—as an understock for modern roses!

Bourbon Roses had nothing to do with Kentucky. The first of the type was sent to France in 1819 from the Isle of Bourbon (now Réunion) in the Indian Ocean off Madagascar. Though it was at first claimed to be a new species, *Rosa bourboniana*, its exact origin is clouded; a similar (if not the same) rose had been growing in the Calcutta Botanic Garden for many years, and a similar type was reported from a neighboring Indian Ocean island, Mauritius (of dodo bird fame). Quite possibly it is an ancient natural hybrid of a Damask and *Rosa chinensis*. The original Bourbon Rose was a semi-double deep pink that flowered repeatedly; plants were vigorous with large, shiny green leaves and purple-tinted canes. Many Bourbon hybrids were named

and sold during the 1800s, the best of which retained the foliage and plant characteristics and the repeat flowering. 'Souvenir de la Malmaison' (1843) and 'Reine Victoria' (1872) are two of the best known; the semi-climber (and completely thornless) 'Zephirine Drouhin' (1868) still is popular in England.

Noisette Roses were the sole American contribution to the 19th century parade of new hybrid types. A hybrid of the China 'Old Blush' and the musk rose, *Rosa moschata*, the first was 'Champneys' Pink Climber'—named by its originator John Champneys of Charleston, South Carolina. His promotion minded neighbor, Philippe Noisette, sent seeds of Champneys' hybrid to France, where the resulting roses became known as Noisettes. Typical Noisette hybrids are either bushy or very vigorous climbers, with large clusters of pale flowers. The most enduring representative, the nostalgic yellow climber 'Mareschal Niel,' resembles the tea roses (see below) far more than it does the Noisettes.

Tea Roses, at the mention of their name, can recall memories of "grandmother's garden" or evoke images of gracious ante-bellum Southern estates. These were the truly everblooming pink, cream, buff, and light yellow roses (usually with weak "necks" below the flowers) that were standard components of 19th and early 20th century rose gardens in mild-winter areas. Countless times referred to as the "aristocrats of the rose world," tea roses left their flower form and overall refinement as legacies to modern roses—along with some of their intolerance of cold winter temperatures.

Very closely related to the China roses, the original tea rose, *Rosa odorata*, reached Europe in 1810. At first it was called the tea-*scented* rose because its fragrance was that of freshly crushed (not dried) tea leaves. Aside from fragrance, however, its semi-double pink flowers were not different enough from the China 'Old Blush' to create any great stir. Its yellow form, variety *ochroleuca*, was sent from China to England in 1824. Basically from these two forms was developed a race of elegant, though tender, garden roses whose popularity lasted for about eighty years until they were superceded by their hardier offspring, the hybrid teas (see page 9).

The importance of the tea and China roses can hardly be overestimated. They are the only source of the capacity for continually repeated bloom found in modern roses, a trait that we take for granted; and they were the first roses to feature the long, pointed bud. Tea roses are extremely long-lived plants, and their foliage is virtually immune to disease. Tenderness is their main drawback.

Hybrid Perpetuals were the 19th century garden and rose show workhorses, particularly in regions where the teas would not thrive. Hybrids they definitely were, encompassing in their ancestries practically all garden roses that had gone before them; but perpetual they were not. The tendency was for a massive spring flowering followed by scattered bloom for the rest of the year, or by a smaller fall burst, or—by nothing. Colors ranged from white through all shades of pink and red to purple, generally in large, full-petalled flowers. Most were capable of forming large plants, often with long, almost climbing canes that produced their best flowers (and their greatest quantity of them) when "pegged down" into a low arch. Several red hybrid Chinas (among them 'Gloire des Rosomanes') and the dark red Portland rose 'Rose du Roi' are supposed to be chiefly responsible for the red shades in the group.

The first roses that could be classed as hybrid perpetuals made their appearance around 1838. From then until just after the turn of the century, the production of these roses occupied all rose breeders of any consequence: the result was more than three thousand of them before their offspring, the hybrid teas (see this page), pushed them out of the gardens. A number of hybrid perpetuals are still around in gardens and catalogues, and one of them is, in some respects, unsurpassed even today. 'General Jacqueminot'—introduced in 1853—was a standard of comparison among red roses for over 60 years and appears somewhere in the ancestry of nearly all modern reds. 'Paul Neyron' is the perfect embodiment of a cabbage rose: big, full of petals, rather flat when open, and pink. For years the rage of the florist trade was 'Mme. Ferdinand Jamin'—but under the name 'American Beauty.' And finally, the superb, pure white 'Frau Karl Druschki,' although introduced back in 1901, still can thrill gardeners with her flawless flowers perfectly displayed against blue-green foliage.

As the hybrid teas (see below) gained in numbers, the hybrid perpetuals lost favor because of two deficiencies in the class: limited color range and lack of a dependable perpetual-flowering inclination. But in comparison to more modern roses, blooms of the best old hybrid perpetuals don't take a back seat.

Hybrid Teas didn't come on the rose scene with a great fanfare. They crept in so imperceptibly that there is some question as to which really was the first. The general formula is hybrid perpetual X tea rose; but because the planting of naturally-pollinated seed was common practice throughout the 19th century, many notable roses have ancestries traceable only on the maternal side (or not at all when hips were gathered at random). Since the hybrid perpetuals were such a melting pot of other roses, a few do show evidence of tea rose background. The designation of 'La France' (1867) as the first hybrid tea, however, marked the beginning of a new era in roses.

To determine early hybrid teas, the best guide is their growth and flowering habits. They definitely were more nearly everblooming and usually grew on smaller but bushier plants than the hybrid perpetuals. Until 1900, the color range in the new class was the same as that found among the hybrid perpetuals, with the addition of creamy yellow tints from the teas. Of the 19th century hybrid teas, in addition to 'La France,' two stand out. 'Mme. Caroline Testout' was a very popular pink because of its beauty and adaptability; it is the rose that once was planted by the thousands along streets

TWO NOSTALGIC HYBRID PERPETUALS still appear frequently in gardens today. 'Frau Karl Druschki' (left) is famous for its pure whiteness, fine form; 'American Beauty' (right) is old cut-flower favorite in rose-red.

of Portland, Oregon. The other is 'Kaiserin Auguste Viktoria,' still an excellent white in climates where its many-petalled flowers can open well.

The year 1900 was a revolutionary turning point for hybrid teas in particular and, indeed, for roses in general: it marked the introduction of Joseph Pernet's 'Soleil d'Or.' From a cross of a purple-red hybrid perpetual and 'Persian Yellow' (a double form of the Austrian Briar Rose, *Rosa foetida*), this was the first large, deep yellow, reasonably hardy bush rose. Up to that time, some tea roses were yellow-flowered, but they were tender plants, their yellow very quickly fading to nearly white. While not strictly a hybrid tea, 'Soleil d'Or' ("Golden Sun") did remarkable things when crossed with them. Suddenly an entirely new palette of colors emerged: bright golden yellow, flame, copper, soft orange, and bicolors of yellow and almost any other color. This was like a transfusion to the tired blood of white, pink, and red-flowered roses. There was, however, a price to pay for the exotic new colors. From *Rosa foetida* these new hybrids inherited a tendency toward poorly-formed blooms (this was the easiest fault to overcome in later hybridizing); lustrous foliage that was particularly susceptible to black spot; and a resentment of pruning, followed by die-back if their canes were severely cut back—by design or by harsh winters. For a number of years, these roses formed a separate sub-class called Pernetianas, but by the 1930s they had been crossed so intensively with hybrid teas that the latter group absorbed them. The glorious Pernetiana colors have permeated all modern rose classes, but so has the hidden legacy of their dislike for pruning shears. Curiously enough, the lavender, mauve, and gray tones that have cropped up in modern roses are derived not just from the purple toned hybrid perpetuals but are a result of interaction with the bright Pernetiana colors.

Polyanthas and Floribundas have a history which parallels that of the hybrid teas. No records exist as to the exact origin of polyantha roses, but it is fairly certain they are derived from the Japanese *Rosa multiflora* and some form of *Rosa chinensis*. The first polyanthas made their appearance in France at about the same time as the hybrid teas. Typically, a polyantha blossoms continually on short, compact plants—blooms are about an inch across, of no special form but in large clusters that may cover the plant. No true polyanthas (that is, exclusively derived from *Rosas multiflora* and *chinensis*) are grown today, but two early polyantha hybrids, 'Cecile Brunner' (1880) and 'Perle d'Or' (1883) have maintained their popularity. They, too, flower in large clusters but have the added feature of shapely blooms on considerably larger plants. The ranunculus-like, salmon-orange 'Margo Koster' is representative of the original type.

A number of other species entered into ancestries of roses classed as polyanthas after 1900. The continuous production of large clusters of small flowers on low plants was the determining factor in the polyantha classification.

Inevitably, these cluster-flowering polyantha types were crossed with hybrid teas to gain better form, increased color range, and still larger flowers on a profuse plant. The Poulsen family in Denmark were pioneers in this endeavor, hoping also to gain hardiness from the polyantha types. It soon became evident, however, that the new hybrids from this union would need some designation other than polyantha or even hybrid polyantha—their larger flowers and shrubbier plants set them definitely apart from the polyantha category. And so the floribundas were born.

Since their inception around 1920, floribundas have been undergoing a continuing refinement. From the single or semi-double, rather informal blooms in large clusters typical of early floribundas, you now have all the hybrid tea colors with the best hybrid tea flower form. In some cases, flowers have become so large and clusters so small that a hybrid tea classification is almost justified.

Grandiflora was the term devised to cover the hybrid tea-floribunda roses which fit neither category. Although the name often has been challenged (British rosarians refer to these roses as "floribundas, hybrid tea type"), it is fairly descriptive of the type. They *are* grand: plants usually are larger and more vigorous than the average hybrid tea, flowers may be as large as hybrid teas but borne in small clusters, and consequently they approach floribunda bloom production. Still the standard for the class is 'Queen Elizabeth,' with her clusters of large, rather informal flowers on a rugged, skyscraping plant. Some hybrid teas have been reclassified to grandiflora because of their vigor and tendency to bloom in small clusters. On the other hand, some grandifloras ('Montezuma' and 'Mount Shasta,' for example) might as well be hybrid teas, for their flowers are as shapely as any and often come one to a stem.

Miniature roses have gone through two widely separated periods of development—first in the years 1820-1850, and more recently since around 1930. Exact origin of the original parent material, *Rosa chinensis minima*, is clouded, but the first plants reached Europe around 1815 —apparently from the island of Mauritius, a British possession in the Indian Ocean. These tiny China roses varied considerably when grown from seed; consequently, most named varieties of the 19th Century ranged through all the China colors from white through red, and from single to very double flowers.

Development of polyantha roses (see this page) eclipsed the miniature rose popularity. But re-discovery, around 1920 in several Swiss villages, of an attractive miniature growing profusely in window boxes again awakened interest in the type. To gain an increased color range and finer flower form, hybridizers have crossed floribundas and polyanthas with miniatures. The result is some variation in dwarfness but perfect replicas of modern hybrid teas.

ROSES OF THE FUTURE

Just as the 19th century saw the rise of hybrid perpetuals and tea roses, and then—at its end—saw them gradually give way to their offspring, the hybrid teas, there is no reason to expect the current hybrid teas not to evolve into still another type of rose that will embody their virtues and bring new ones as well. The grandifloras give a clue to one course of development roses will take—indeed, are taking already. Plants will be exceptionally vigorous and fast growing (although not necessarily huge), and flowers will be plentiful enough for a good garden display and for cutting to decorate the home. Plants also will be tough enough to step out of the traditional "rose bed" and function as flowering shrubs and hedges.

And there will be even more dramatic developments. A number of hybridizers are working patiently toward two utopian goals: plants that will be immune to foliage diseases, and plants that will go through the coldest of winters with no protection and little or no damage from the cold. Already there are hybrids which fit part of the bill. By no means new (1918) is the rampant climber 'Mermaid,' which has the desired foliage—but she is more tender than most hybrid teas and is useless for further hybridizing because of sterility. 'Therese Bugnet' will endure winter unprotected in her native Alberta, Canada, and come up smiling in spring, but her leaves may be troubled by the usual hybrid tea foliage ills. And neither of the roses possesses the sculptured beauty of a hybrid tea blossom. These, however, are but two examples of a steadily growing number. A large, untapped reservoir of species waits to be used in experimental breeding—particularly those native to North America, none of which has played a part in the development of modern roses.

Probably the most visually appealing successes in this direction have come from Wilhelm Kordes in Germany. From an artificially created species, *Rosa kordesii*, he has bred a series of shrub and climbing roses that are hardier than the average hybrid tea, have better foliage, and are strong growers. Flowers in some like 'Leverkusen' and 'Zweibrucken' approach those of hybrid teas in size and form.

Progress may be slow: some of the best potential parent material is incompatible with hybrid teas; or their offspring is sterile; or the desired traits get lost before flowers are improved; or several generations of breeding produce no flower improvement. But with geneticists and knowledgeable hybridizers working toward the ultimate foolproof rose, development is bound to be faster than was the improvement made in the 19th century by sowing naturally formed hips and *hoping* for some exciting differences. Eventually, from careful planning, we'll have roses that will thrive with the same care from Alaska to Florida.

A FEW ROSE TERMS TO KNOW

As you read about roses, you are bound to run across terms that have special meaning when applied to rose growing. The following list explains the most familiar jargon words of the rose world.

Bud. This may have several meanings. The most obvious is reference to the unopened flower. It also can mean the growth bud or eye found where leaves join stems. For a propagator of roses, to *bud* is to take the growth eye and develop a plant from it by a special grafting technique (see page 30).

Bud Union. On a commercially propagated rose bush, this is the part of the plant where top growth joins with the understock (see below), generally 1-3 inches above the roots. It is an enlarged "knob" from which all major stems grow (and it grows larger each year).

Canes. The principal stems which grow from the bud union (or from very low on the bush) and form the plant's structure.

Hip. The seed pod that can form after a flower's petals fall if the bloom was pollinated (as happens naturally very often). Many turn brilliant autumn colors in fall and can be very decorative.

Plant patent. Most new rose introductions are "patented." This means that the patent holder and the rose's originator receive a small percentage from the sale of each plant until the patent expires after 21 years. This is a strong guarantee that plants you purchase will be true to name and well grown. It also stimulates research and hybridizing, as the hybridizer is assured of some financial reward for his work.

Sport. A change in growth habit or flower color that may occur suddenly on an established variety. Climbing forms of bush varieties typify a growth sport; 'Flaming Peace,' a red and gold bicolor, is an example of a color sport which was found on a plant of the normally light yellow and pink 'Peace.'

Standard. Commonly called "tree rose," the standard is just a rose bush budded high on an understock stem (see page 73). Sizes range from miniature standards on 12-inch stems through 24-inch patio standards, 36-inch regular standards to occasional 6-foot weeping standards onto which are budded flexible-caned ramblers.

Sucker. Any growth that arises from below the bud union on a budded plant. This growth is that of the understock and should be removed (see page 26).

Understock. The rose that furnished the root system to plants propagated by budding (see page 30).

The Art of Growing Roses

Roses may thrive in a variety of soils. This fact underscores one of the plant's virtues: rugged adaptability. Yet the roots of a rose plant do have a few definite preferences that, when satisfied, can make the difference between indifferent and superior performance. Before you plant your new roses you should know what these preferences are, what *your* soil is like, and how it can be handled to satisfy the roses' needs.

SOILS AND THEIR IMPROVEMENT

Regardless of what kind of soil you have, it is composed of mineral particles formed by the action of weather on some sort of rock. Because these particles do not fit together exactly, there are spaces between them. When soil is dry, the spaces are filled with air; when water is added to soil, however, it moves downward, filling the spaces with water and coating each particle. As water continues to move down through soil, air re-enters the spaces vacated by water, although a water film remains around each soil grain.

This interchange between water and air in the soil is vital to rose roots. In order to reach their best possible growth, roses need a soil that is moist but that drains well enough that the soil's natural air spaces do not remain filled with water for any length of time. Roots need oxygen in order to function properly; in a waterlogged soil the oxygen supply is cut off and the rose roots actually suffocate.

Without going into a detailed breakdown of soil classification, let's consider that most soils will be basically clay, sand, or some gradation between the two. What determines the clayeyness or sandiness of a soil is the size of its individual particles.

Clay soils are composed of minute, flattened particles that group together very tightly, producing a compact, heavy soil. Pore space between clay particles is microscopic, so that water drains very slowly through them and air space is severely limited. Despite the fact that individual clay particles are well supplied with nutrients essential for plant growth, plant roots have a difficult time penetrating very far in this type of compact soil.

Sandy soils contain the largest particles (more than 25 times the size of the largest clay particles) and have correspondingly large pore spaces between. They drain well (so are well-aerated) but retain moisture and dissolved nutrients so poorly that plants need more frequent attention than they do when planted in clay.

Loam, the happy medium so often mentioned in garden books, may contain soil particles intermediate in size between clay and sand, and/or may contain a mixture of particle sizes. Drainage, aeration, and moisture retention of loam also are a compromise between the extremes of clay and sand.

How can you tell what sort of soil you have? You can look, feel, and dig. When dry, clay soils usually will crack; sandy ones won't. When they're wet, clays can feel almost greasy but sand will feel gritty. Finally, dig

TEST SOIL DRAINAGE *even before you purchase roses. Dig a foot-deep hole, fill it with water; check an hour later to see how much (if any) is left. This will tell you if any special drainage provisions may be needed.*

about a foot-deep hole and fill it with water; if there still is water in the hole an hour later, you can be sure your soil is more clay-like than sandy, and probably will require some special attention to improve its drainage (see page 14).

How Deep Is Your Soil?

You should have no trouble discovering whether your soil tends to be sandy, clayey, or somewhere in between. The next discovery you'll have to make is the depth of your soil. Take a spade or spading fork and dig a trial hole about two feet deep in the area where you want to plant your roses. With any luck, you will encounter no obstruction—and neither will rose roots. Complications you might encounter close to the soil surface are these: hardpan (a layer of impervious soil, usually found only in low-rainfall regions), bedrock (or at least the parent material of your soil, such as limestone or sandstone), or occasional boulders too large to remove. Where a hardpan prevails, you sometimes can break through it (if it is not too thick) and laboriously but successfully remove it from a planting bed. Often beneath it will be subsoil which will drain adequately. With bedrock near the surface, you'll have to construct raised planting beds; these, with the combined depth of native topsoil and new soil added to the bed, should provide about a two-foot depth for your roses' roots.

Sometimes soil around new homes may have been compacted by heavy equipment used in construction,

HUSKY BARE-ROOT *plant shows qualities to look for: strong, extensive root system; several canes from bud union.*

and also may contain quantities of construction debris (especially close around the house). A deep digging (with the aeration it brings) plus incorporation of organic materials may be all you'll need to do in a light to medium soil. With compacted heavy clay soil, however, it probably would be easier and more successful for you to make raised planting beds.

Improving Your Soil

Knowing your basic soil type gives you the theme upon which you make the variations to best satisfy your roses. And a component that can beneficially vary all soils is organic matter—decomposing plant and animal remains.

In clay soils, organic materials act as wedges between the tiny, compacted soil particles while the more fully decomposed parts of the organic matter (called *humus*) are sticky and hold together groups of particles in small crumbs. This wedging and aggregation action loosens up the clay and allows freer penetration of air and water. In sandy soils, organic materials fill in the large spaces between sand grains and act as sponges to hold moisture and nutrients, reducing the too-rapid drainage. And keep in mind the human benefit of added organic matter: it makes it easier for you, the gardener, to dig and cultivate.

You have a wide open choice of organic materials that will improve your soil. The easiest to get (but more expensive) are commercially packaged items such as peat moss, steer manure, redwood sawdust, or leaf mold. Very likely you will be able to locate suitable waste materials in your area—inexpensive if you are able to haul them away. Grape or apple pomace, rice hulls, ground corncobs, wood by-products such as sawdust and shavings, mushroom compost, spent hops, various animal manures are just a small sampling of materials you might find. If you maintain a compost heap, you need not search beyond your own back yard.

Whatever you add to improve your soil, try to use enough to comprise at least 25 per cent of the amount of soil you're preparing. This means that for the average spade's depth bite (8-9 inches) ideally you should add at least four inches of organic material. For easier work and more uniform results, dig in not more than a two-inch layer of organic materials at one time. If you don't plan to improve the soil of the entire rose bed but prefer to add organic materials to each hole at planting time, be sure to read the cautions mentioned in the next column. In addition, remember that a planting hole well fortified with organic matter can be a trap where surrounding soil is poorly drained; each hole becomes a suffocating bathtub for roots. See page 15 for tips on how to improve poorly drained soil.

If you have a heavy clay soil, there are two other widely sold and relatively inexpensive materials that you can add in addition to organic matter to improve the soil structure. Both gypsum and lime, when added to clay, will cause the particles to group together into larger crumbs, improving drainage and workability. Which one you use depends upon the acidity or alkalinity of your soil (see page 25). If you have neutral to alkaline soil, use gypsum; sprinkle it on the soil surface so that it resembles a light snowfall, then dig it in. For acid soils, use lime in the amount recommended by your county agricultural agent, remembering that roses prefer a slightly acid soil (about pH 6.0-6.8).

Why Prepare Early?

If you know several months in advance that you are going to plant roses, you have the opportunity to prepare soil early so that it will have a chance to mellow and settle in the meantime. This also makes the planting more pleasurable when the roses arrive: you then don't have to spend time adding organic amendments to the soil while the roses wait. For fall planting, prepare your soil in the summer; but if you will be planting in winter or spring see that you prepare your soil in the early fall at the latest. After you have spaded and incorporated organic matter, the soil level will be several inches above the surrounding soil, but by the time rose planting season arrives it will have settled so that you easily can gauge the proper planting depth.

Advance preparation gives you the chance to use a much greater variety of organic soil amendments than you could use at the time you plant your roses. Fresh animal manures (which will burn newly-planted rose roots with their excessive nitrogen content) and undecomposed organic materials (which temporarily take nitrogen from the soil to aid their breakdown) usually will mellow sufficiently within several months after having been added to the soil so that you can then plant with safety.

If you choose to improve the soil at the time you plant new roses, be sure to use organic materials that contain enough nitrogen for their decomposition (such as nitrogen-fortified wood products), or materials that already are significantly decomposed (compost or leaf mold, for example) or peat moss which breaks down so slowly that there is no significant nitrogen depletion. Don't risk using animal manure in a planting hole where it would come into direct contact with roots unless you are sure the manure is thoroughly aged.

Steps Toward Better Drainage

If your soil has flunked the drainage test described on page 13, you would be wise to make some special preparations for the planting area before you begin to improve the soil. Even the most ideal, porous soil will not grow roses well if the subsoil and soil surrounding the bed are of heavy clay that will not allow water to escape from the area. Without making provisions for drainage away from the site, you essentially plant your roses in undrained containers.

What should you do for a poorly-drained soil? If your garden is level, a raised bed is your best solution. Plan to have the soil surface of the raised bed one foot above the normal grade. Dig organic materials and gypsum or lime (see page 14) into the top two feet of native soil, then add the additional soil to raise the bed and dig it (along with more organic matter) into the native soil beneath. Allow a couple of months time for the bed to settle before you plant it. If settling is too great, add more new soil and dig it into the bed.

Where soil is poorly drained and the garden is on a slope (or if land near the proposed planting site slopes away from it), you can plant at ground level if you install drainage pipes or tile beneath the beds. Then, when water percolates through the carefully prepared rose bed soil, it enters the pipes and moves out of the bed *if* it can empty into a spot lower than the level of the pipe. This can be either of two ways—draining downslope or draining into a sump.

Installation of pipe is simply an efficient modification of an ancient drainage principle: Roman swampland was drained for cultivation by the digging of deep and broad trenches to collect water that saturated the top several feet of soil. The diagrams below show how to place the drainage pipes. After they are in place, prepare the soil above them with organic materials, gypsum or lime (see page 14), then let it settle before planting.

If the slope of your land is something steeper than gentle, you might prefer to terrace your plantings. This will give you a level planting surface, yet water will drain away down the slope. Wood, concrete blocks, brick, or even stone (if you're ambitious and skillful) all make fine retaining walls for terraced beds. Build the retaining walls first, then fill in behind with soil liberally mixed with organic materials. Especially if your native soil drains poorly, you'd be wise to incorporate several "weep holes" at the base of each retaining wall; these will allow excess water to drain easily out of the bed instead of collecting at the lowest part and building up pressure against the retaining wall.

Older gardening books — particularly those from England—describe a laborious but effective way to prepare soil deeply. Called double digging, it aerates and improves the subsoil—from about the 12-inch to the 24-inch depth. Since rose roots will (and should) penetrate deeply, this sort of soil preparation is to their advantage. However, there is a *reasonably* simple way to do it—at least a less cumbersome method than old English gardeners recommend. First dig out the top foot of soil from the proposed rose bed and lay this soil to one side (put it on some sort of tarpaulin or plastic cloth if you have to pile it on lawn or a loose paving material). Then, thoroughly dig into the next foot of soil your organic materials (and gypsum or lime if your soil needs it). Finally, return to the bed the soil you had laid aside, digging into this top layer the same materials you just have added to the subsoil.

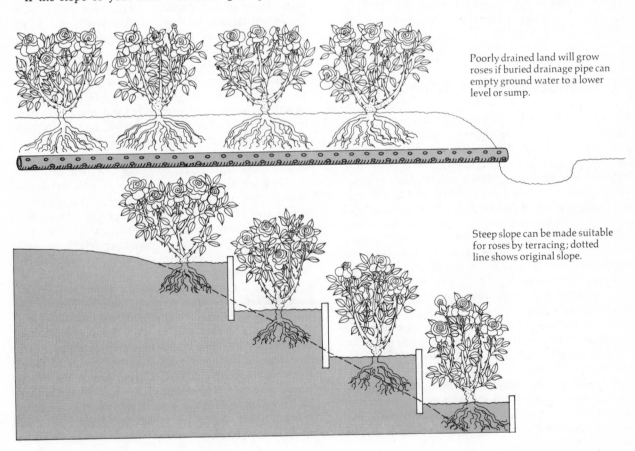

Poorly drained land will grow roses if buried drainage pipe can empty ground water to a lower level or sump.

Steep slope can be made suitable for roses by terracing; dotted line shows original slope.

TIPS FOR SELECTING ROSES

Now that you understand your soil and have made any necessary adjustments so that it should grow roses well, you can concentrate on selecting and purchasing the plants.

Most roses will grow in nearly all climates, but some varieties do better than others in particular regions. For your greatest pleasure you should first find out what sorts are reputed to perform well in your area, and one of the best sources of this information is a local rose grower. The nearest Consulting Rosarian of the American Rose Society (see page 35) can draw upon his years of reading and experience to help guide your choices. Even over-the-back-fence conversation with your neighbors may disclose at least a limited list of sure performers for your area. Many places have municipal gardens and specific rose test gardens where newer varieties plus satisfactory old favorites are displayed. Often, visits to one of these gardens will show you which varieties are suited to your climate. For vital statistics on 220 rose varieties (and color photographs of 53 favorites), browse through pages 34-63.

If you have no access to local information, you can get a general indication of widespread merit by checking the ratings assigned to varieties in the "Handbook for Selecting Roses," a buying guide compiled by the American Rose Society. These ratings are based on nationwide evaluations and are on a scale running from 1 to 10; any rose that scores 8.0 or better is likely to turn in a satisfactory performance in all parts of the country.

WHERE TO BUY NEW ROSES

Avoiding the temptation to buy roses is not easy. Most nurseries have them throughout the year: first in bare-root planting season; then growing in containers during the remaining months. Large commercial rose growers advertise their wares widely with enticing color photographs. And if you escape these inducements, very likely you'll find packaged bare-root plants offered for sale in supermarkets. You may wonder which sources will give you the best plants for your money—and the answer is that any of them *can*. What you have to do is consider the advantages and drawbacks in each situation.

If you order from a specialist rose nursery, your only disadvantage is that you can't personally select the plants you receive. But because their business depends entirely on your satisfaction they will ship nothing but first class plants. Aside from convenience (you just wait for the plants to come to you) mail-order rose specialists are the readiest sources for the newest hybrids. Some of these nurseries also make a point of carrying old or unusual roses that almost always are not available locally. Catalogues usually will offer a greater selection from which you can choose than any other source. They may not, however, always carry the middle-aged and old favorite hybrid teas whose low individual prices can't justify producing them in quantity and allocating to them colorful catalogue space.

Catalogue shopping can be a truly exciting experience. The descriptions—if not sufficiently tantalizing in themselves— often will be accompanied by irresistable color photographs. Remember, though, in your eagerness to throw all caution to the winds and send for *every* rose you want, the guidelines outlined on page 35 for selecting satisfactory varieties for your area.

Although planting times vary from fall through spring (see page 20) throughout the country, the earlier you place your order the more certain you are of receiving your first choices. Most catalogues are ready for mailing sometime in the fall. No matter when you plant, you would be wise to place your order soon after catalogues arrive—ideally before the December holidays. Whatever your preferred bare-root planting season is, ask for delivery of plants early in that season; this will give new plants the longest possible growing season in your garden, and is good insurance against your choices being sold out. If, however, you find yourself placing a late order, you are likely to be happier if you list a few acceptable substitutions rather than leaving the choice of possible alternates to the seller. This way you avoid receiving as a substitute a rose you already have or one you don't care for. Many large mail-order rose growers (even those in warm-winter areas) have cold-storage facilities that enable them to ship you well-ripened, dormant bushes at the best planting time for your region.

The particular roses stocked by your nearby nursery depends on your nurseryman, but typically he will have the new and recent All-America winners (see page 35) as well as the standard, time-tested and proven varieties. In addition, if he's on his toes, he will be sure to stock any roses that are especially suited to your regional climate regardless of their performance in other dissimilar areas. Usually, his bare-root roses will be heeled into beds of sawdust so that you can pick out plants having good, healthy canes. This way, if you see that a plant's root system has been badly damaged in digging or shipping, you can select another one on the spot. Since his livelihood depends on your return business and word-of-mouth endorsement, he's just as interested in your satisfaction as you are.

Perhaps the source of greatest concern is the local supermarket. For convenience it can't be beaten. Although the assortment of varieties will not be exceptional, typically they will be the old favorites of past decades, as well as current top-rated patented roses. Sometimes a disappointingly high percentage of these roses are incorrectly labeled. Unfortunately, there's no sure way to determine this until they leaf out and bloom. So if you are looking for a particular variety, you have a much better chance for satisfaction from mail order specialists or retail nurseries.

BARE-ROOT QUALITY STANDARDS

Nearly all roses sold bare-root are "two-year-old, field-grown plants." This means that the roots are about two years old and the canes somewhat younger (see page 35). For these bare-root plants, the American Association of Nurserymen has established quality standards, designated by numbers. Consequently, when a nursery advertises No. 1, No. 1½, or No. 2 plants, you know in advance what sort of plants to expect. For the principal types of roses sold—hybrid tea, grandiflora, floribunda, polyantha, and climber—here are the specifications for these grades; in all cases, the canes measured to determine the grade should originate within three inches of the bud union where top growth joins rootstock.

No. 1 grade. Hybrid teas and grandifloras must have three or more strong canes, at least two of which are 18 inches or more in length. Canes on No. 1 floribundas should meet the same specifications, except that they need be only 15 inches long. Number 1 polyanthas must have four or more canes of 12 inches or longer. Climbing roses need three or more canes of at least 24 inches.

No. 1½ grade. Hybrid teas and grandifloras need two or more strong canes of at least 15 inches long. Floribundas should have two canes that measure 14 inches or more. Number 1½ climbers must have two 18-inch canes. Polyanthas that do not meet number 1 standards are not graded.

No. 2 grade. Hybrid teas and grandifloras—the only types you're ever likely to find in this grade—need have only 2 canes of 12 inches or longer. These plants are strictly a gamble, since they may be the runts of the 2-year-old field which produced the No. 1 plants also being offered.

Measurements expressed in the grading standards are for the plant as it is dug from the field. Very often the grower, packager, or nurseryman will reduce the cane length for more convenient shipping or handling, but the cane diameter will indicate to you whether the plant originally qualified for the grade indicated. Some of the smaller-growing roses (such as 'Snowbird' or 'Sarabande') may appear to just barely make the No. 1 standards, but this size is natural: never will they have canes equal to those of husky giants like 'Queen Elizabeth.'

The chief gamble you take with these plants, however, is that you can't see their root systems: inevitably the roots are enclosed in long, narrow bags containing a moistened fibrous material, the bag tied just below the bud union. The canes are always on view—either dipped in wax to retain moisture or swathed in a transparent plastic bag for the same reason. Assuming the canes appear in good condition—not shriveled or discolored, eyes plump and ready to grow but not growing—you can consider the plant a good risk. Sometimes in the digging or in the packaging, however, major roots will be broken, and you won't discover this until you unwrap them just before planting. Such roses may take an extra year or two, while they rebuild their lost root systems, before showing their best in your garden. One general tip for buying packaged rose plants: do it while they are still *new* on the supermarket shelves. Those with plastic-wrapped canes are well protected against the drying indoor atmosphere, but because the plastic acts as a miniature greenhouse, these plants often begin to grow soon after being set out on the shelves. Even if you're not prepared to plant them when they appear in the market, *you* can more carefully watch over the packaged roses at home until the planting moment arrives. If you can't plant them right away, see instructions on page 18 for holding bare root plants.

Should you, despite all precautions, find yourself with sprouted plants to set out, just cut the shoots back to ¼-inch stubs. This will prevent the new shoots from using up moisture in the plants before roots are established enough to replenish it.

CHOICE OF BEST plants is yours when you shop for bare-root roses at nursery. Look for plants like one on page 13.

Container-Grown Roses

Throughout the year many retail nurseries have selections of roses growing and blooming in containers. Generally these plants are somewhat more expensive than the same varieties bare-root because of the labor required to plant and care for them at the nursery.

Of the several advantages to buying these roses, perhaps the most compelling one is that you can see that the plant is alive and healthy and you can check its flowers (especially important if the variety is new to you). You will be able to tell if its color and form are what you prefer, and you can tell something about its foliage color and disease resistance. If any roses in your garden have died over the winter, this is a quick way to fill in the gaps; and, of course, it puts instant color into a new rose garden. The best time to go shopping for container-grown roses is during their first flush of bloom in spring, since flowers are often at their best then, and the selection of varieties will be the greatest.

What, then, are the risks in buying container-grown roses? As with packaged supermarket plants, you cannot see the root systems. But here you *can* see and judge the plant's health and vigor, and almost always you will be correct to assume that the robust container plant is just as healthy beneath the soil surface. More and more container-grown plants of all kinds are being potted in very porous soil mixtures; so be especially sure you plant these roses in soil which will allow excess water to drain off easily (see pages 12-15 for preparing soil).

Unless the nurseryman makes a specialty of container-grown roses, you probably will find the selection more limited than the bare-root offering. And rare is the nursery which will ship these plants—other than, perhaps, a local delivery by truck.

If you go shopping for blooming roses in containers, keep these three points in mind:

• Buy your roses in the largest container offered. Best are 3 or 5 gallon cans or their equivalent volume in wooden tubs, crates, or paper pots. By all means steer clear of roses in gallon cans or small flower pots, whose roots may have been pruned severely to fit into the small containers.

• Purchase only bushes that were planted earlier in the year from bare-root stock. Under nursery conditions, container-grown roses held over from previous years inevitably suffer from their prolonged confinement. Telltale signs of such older plants are pruning scars from past years (often accompanied by slight dieback), dead canes or branches with twiggy growth attached, or many small branches that have accumulated from lack of pruning.

• Do your shopping before summer heat arrives. Not only do nursery roses look their worst then, but also summer is the most difficult time of year to establish a new plant in your garden. Roses kept in cans *through* a hot summer may suffer from insufficient water or fertilizer, or from burned root tips that touched the sides of metal containers. And if they have grown well they are likely to be pot bound by mid-summer. Root bound roses often never outgrow the confines of the original root ball after being planted out in the garden. The result often is unsatisfactory performance.

Preparation for Planting

Before you even pick up a shovel with your new rose plants in hand, examine the new bushes carefully. They should measure up to the grade advertised by the seller and not be weak appearing or spindly; the root system should not have been badly cut up in the harvesting or broken in shipping. Sometimes you will find slight root breakage in packaging and shipping, but it should not be excessive. Always cut back any damaged roots with a sharp, clean pair of pruning shears before you plant.

Occasionally, plants shipped during severe winter weather become frozen in transit. Freezing breaks up the cell structure of the canes and usually causes the roots to turn black. Even if you carefully thaw them, these plants are practically worthless and should be replaced. Plants that have been overheated in transit will have live roots but black canes. Very rarely will you receive a diseased or dead plant.

Any time quality of the plants you receive does not measure up to what you expected, you immediately should get in touch with the nurseryman or mail-order specialist about possible replacement. But give the seller the benefit of the doubt. Reputable rose specialists and nurserymen are eager to see that you get top quality stock and often will replace plants even when damage was beyond their control.

When weather and soil conditions permit, the ideal moment to plant new roses is as soon as you get them. If you cannot plant right away, you should do one of two things to keep the new arrivals in a fresh but dormant condition until you can plant them:

1) Heeling in—the simplest and best treatment for holding new roses—is possible only when you are able to work the soil. In a shaded place dig a trench that has one slanted side, lay the plants against this slant with their roots at the trench's bottom, then cover the roots *and* canes with soil, thoroughly watering them in. In a cool shaded spot these roses will hold longer before breaking dormancy than they would where exposed to warming sunlight. Even so, you should plant them at the very first opportunity, for root growth may begin while heeled in, and the less of this there is to disturb during planting, the better.

2) An alternate method, whenever heeling is impossible, is to pack the roots in some sort of moisture-retentive material and set new plants in a cool (but not freezing) place, such as a garage or basement. Very often mail order roses and even plants from the nearby nursery will have their roots packed in moist peat moss, sawdust, perlite, or similar absorbent material. All you have to do, then, is remove the packing, soak it in water, squeeze out surplus moisture so it is damp but doesn't drip, and repack it around the rose roots. Check

BARE-ROOT PLANTING *begins with hole large enough to hold roots without crowding (left); mix in soil amendments now if you didn't prepare soil early. Make a firm cone of soil (right) in hole and spread roots over it.*

CHECK SOIL LEVEL *with stick placed across hole (left); this positions bud union (see box on page 20). Fill hole nearly full with soil, water it in (center). Then, mound plant with soil and keep it there until growth begins.*

these plants often to make sure the packing does not dry out, and add more water if necessary.

Some roses may come to you completely encased in plastic bags or sheeting that retain moisture well around roots and canes. If you leave the bags unopened and keep them in a cool, dark place, they will hold safely for a week to ten days. But if you have to hold these plants indoors where it is warmer be sure to remove the plastic from around the canes; moisture will condense on the inside of the plastic and, combined with warmth, can make miniature greenhouses out of the package and cause the plants to start growth. In this case you will need to get some peat moss, sawdust, or other moisture holding material to pack around the roots.

Whatever holding method you use, don't let the rose roots dry out, even for a short time. Desiccated canes often can be revived and at least will be replaced in time by new ones. But the plant has only one root system.

With any bare-root rose bush, it is a good idea to soak the entire plant in water for a few hours (but not more than 24) just prior to planting. This will help restore moisture to all the plant tissues at once. Then, after you plant it, cover the canes with a mound of moist soil or other moisture-holding material for a week or two to keep canes from drying while the roots are establishing themselves. Gradually and carefully remove this mound as new growth begins.

HOW DEEP TO PLANT

Where there's no need for winter protection, there's no question about planting depth: after soil has settled from the planting operation, the bud union should be about an inch above soil level. But in cold-winter areas, controversy rages. There, rosarians have planted with bud unions as much as 2 inches below soil level. If canes were frozen to the ground in a severe winter, they reasoned, at least the bud union might live to grow a new plant. But this approach has two drawbacks. Buried bud unions grow few new canes from the union itself but, instead, form false bud unions low on the canes above soil surface. And often the bud union will form its own roots which do not supplement the understock but eventually starve it to extinction. The resulting old, own-root plant rarely is as vigorous as the same rose still growing on an understock.

Nowadays, many rosarians even in frigid Midwestern states are planting with bud unions anywhere from an inch above the soil surface to even with it, then *carefully* applying winter protection each year. The result is a plant that will form more new canes from the bud union each year than will those with buried unions. And in sub-zero areas this is an advantage, as roses often must replace annually top growth killed over winter.

When to Do Bare-Root Planting

Technically, you can plant bare-root roses at any time during the dormant season when soil is not frozen. For much of the South, Southwest, and West Coast, this means January and February with the possibility of March before dormancy is broken. In these regions, where winter lows seldom reach 10° above zero, the sooner you can plant, the better. Where winter cold is capricious—alternating with spells of warmer weather —and where freezing typically settles in for several months, you probably will prefer (if not be compelled) to plant either in fall or spring. The one advantage of fall planting is that the new plant may have about a five month lead over the spring-planted bush in establishing its roots. In severe winters, though, little if any root growth will take place, and you run a risk of losing a new plant even though you protect it well. A premature spring warm spell may be just enough to break a new plant's dormancy and leave it vulnerable to subsequent freezes. The only real drawback to spring planting is that top growth and root growth begin almost simultaneously. If early spring weather is unseasonably warm, the top may temporarily outstrip the roots. These plants will need close attention to be sure roots always have enough water.

In cold-winter areas, experienced growers in your region can give you the best advice for local planting time. Rose-growing friends, a reliable nurseryman who deals in roses, or the nearest Consulting Rosarian (see page 35) should be able to advise you well. Generally, if you are ordering from a large specialist rose nursery that has cold storage facilities, you'd be wise to order for early spring planting; the grower can hold the new bushes over the winter under ideal conditions.

WATERING

There is no mystery surrounding how and how much to water roses. Yet a lack of sufficient water probably is the major cause of less than satisfactory results from roses—especially newly planted ones. The rose is a thirsty plant. Although the bushes usually will survive when only skimpily supplied with water, they will perform at their vigorous best only when their roots are kept moist during the growing season. Even in regions where spring and summer rainfall is frequent, don't assume that these showers will completely satisfy your roses' needs.

Just how much water roses should receive can be stated only in relation to what sort of soil you have. First, remember that although rose roots should be kept damp, the soil around them should never be saturated for any length of time. Such saturation excludes vital oxygen from the soil (see page 12), and roots need oxygen as much as they do water in order to carry on the plant's life processes.

Watering to the full depth of their roots will produce the best results from your roses. This means a water penetration to at least 16-18 inches. Frequent but light waterings will not penetrate very far below the soil surface, encouraging the network of feeder roots to grow in this shallow, moist zone. Concentrated close to the surface, they are subject to injury by cultivating or weeding, may be burned by fertilizers, or may be damaged if this soil layer dries out.

But how can you tell if your watering has penetrated deeply enough? The surest way is to conduct a simple test to determine your soil's ability to absorb water; you can time subsequent water applications to match your soil's capacity. Begin by watering your roses as you normally would (or, if you are growing your first roses, pick an arbitrary amount of time—say, 15 minutes). Then, on the day after you water, dig down about 18 inches to actually see how far your watering penetrated. If you discover, for example, that half an hour's irrigation wetted only the top 10 inches of soil you will know that your watering time should be doubled in order to moisten the entire root zone.

Since water penetration varies according to soil type, the University of California conducted studies to accurately determine rates of absorption in the different types. These studies disclosed that 1 cubic inch of water on top of the ground will wet directly downward 12 inches in sandy soil, 6-10 inches in loam, or 4-5 inches in clay. This means that to wet the soil to a 2-foot depth in a 2-foot-square basin requires 5 gallons of water in a sandy soil, 7.6 gallons in loam, and 13.2 gallons in clay. Few people would want to take the time to water their roses by the gallon, but these figures point out that a trickle from the hose in clay soil will take a longer time to produce the necessary volume than will the same flow in sand.

After asking how much water roses need, the next most common question concerns how often they should be watered. And here again the answer is a relative one, depending on your soil. As the University of California studies imply, sandy soil absorbs water quickly whereas clay soils are slow to take it in. Water is exhausted much more quickly, however, in sand than in clay. In sandy soil, then, you will spend fewer hours at a time watering your roses than you would in clay but you'll return to do it more often. For example, during "average" springtime weather you may have to water your roses about every 5 days in sand, every week to week-and-a-half in loam, but only every other week in clay. Daytime temperatures, amount of sunlight, and wind action (all of which influence the transpiration rate) and the presence or lack of a mulch will vary these generalizations. During hot, dry spells, for example, you will need to water at closer intervals; a day of hot, dry wind will cause leaves to lose a great deal of water through transpiration, requiring prompt replacement in the root zone.

An easy check for need of water can be done this way: take a trowel and open up a small hole in the soil,

then feel with your finger to see if soil is moist (not soggy) three inches below the surface. If it is damp, wait; but if soil is dry, water again for your usual amount of time.

If you live in a summer-rainfall region, a rain gauge placed in your rose bed (but out of reach of any sprinklers) will give you a fairly accurate—and perhaps surprising—record of how much or little water nature is providing.

Don't overlook dormant season watering, just because your roses are standing still. Continue to water, but on a more limited program, as long as soil is not frozen.

How to Apply Water

When it comes to *how* to water your roses, you have a choice between irrigating and sprinkling. Most successful rose growers in summer-rainfall regions will vote for some form of irrigation as the better of the two. There, rain washes foliage often enough, but may not be enough to keep roots moist. In dry-summer areas, many rosarians get best results from regular irrigation augmented by periodic sprinklings of the entire rose garden.

Particularly in smoggy or dusty areas, you will do your plants a great favor if you wash off their foliage every week or so. (As an added bonus this also will wash away some insect pests, notably aphids and spider mites.) But for this, pick an early morning of what promises to be a sunny day, so that leaves will be dry by nightfall.

You can choose from among countless ways to go about irrigating—from the simple basin around each plant to elaborate systems of canals that link all basins together. But best results usually follow when each plant has its own basin so that irrigation water can be concentrated in the plant's root zone. The basic basin is simply an earthen dike around each plant and anywhere from two to six inches high; make it about 20 inches or more across. Its rim should encircle the bush just beyond the drip line (or the anticipated drip line of a newly planted bush). For established plantings don't try to make the basin ridges by scraping soil from the rose bed. Instead, haul in enough soil from another part of the garden. Any disturbance of the soil surface near the rose plant could damage some of its feeder roots which lie just beneath the soil surface.

If you think a rose planting will be unattractive with each bush growing out of a separate crater-like basin, this appearance can be modified greatly by using a mulch (see page 22) inside the basins and on the ground between.

A more formal, structured appearance may be created by making the basin sides of brick or concrete block. This is particularly useful in sandy soils which cannot compact well enough to make very stable ridges, but it is useful anywhere you want a basin whose sides will never need repair. If your native soil is stony, you could employ some of the larger stones to make naturalistic basins that will be as permanent as brick or concrete. Gardeners in arid regions where flood irrigation is employed for all plants often entirely surround their rose beds with a concrete curbing to contain the water.

How to get water to your roses in basins is only an efficiency problem for you to solve. For just a few bushes, the simplest method is to move the hose from plant to plant until all are watered. You can even cut down time on this method by employing one or more "Y" connections at the end of your principal hose, with secondary hoses going to more than one bush at a time. To avoid having soil scoured by water from the hose end, you can buy a "bubbler" attachment that diffuses the water through many small holes to reduce its force without cutting down the volume. An old sock or garden glove tied over the hose end accomplishes the same purpose.

Plastic pipe offers several possibilities for designing effective irrigation systems; all you need to put one together are a saw and either glue or special fittings, yet these systems can be as permanent as steel pipe. The accompanying diagrams illustrate three simple irrigation devices made entirely from plastic. The perforated pipe arrangement and the one using "spaghetti" tubing are designed for resting on the soil surface and could be obscured by a mulch. The system with open risers would be buried an inch or two beneath the surface.

In cold winter areas where water in the pipes would freeze, you'll have to lay it so that it can be completely drained in fall. Otherwise they should be taken up and stored indoors every winter.

MULCHING

Hand in hand with watering comes the subject of mulches and mulching, for mulches are as effective as a cloudy day in conserving water you have given plants.

In addition to being practical, most mulches will put the finishing touch on the appearance of your rose garden: the wall-to-wall carpeting beneath the bushes.

Basically, a mulch is any material which you put on top of the soil to hold back moisture loss and to keep soil cool. You can use a tremendous variety of materials —from organics (such as animal manures) to inorganic ones like stones. Whatever you choose, its primary function is to retard evaporation from soil so that roots do not experience rapid and severe alternations between wet and dry, cool and hot. And this is the other immediate benefit of a mulch: it keeps soil cool, simply by putting a barrier between warming sun's rays and the ground surface. Feeder roots close to the surface benefit greatly from this moderation. For this reason, however, rose growers in regions where soil temperature remains below freezing during much of the winter usually prefer to delay mulching until the soil has warmed up from its winter chill. Applying a mulch as soon as spring arrives may slow root growth by keeping soil too cool.

Generally, a mulch an inch or two thick also will turn out to be an effective weed control agent, particularly if the ground has been weeded thoroughly sometime before laying the mulch. Any weed seeds that germinate in the mulch can be pulled from it easily.

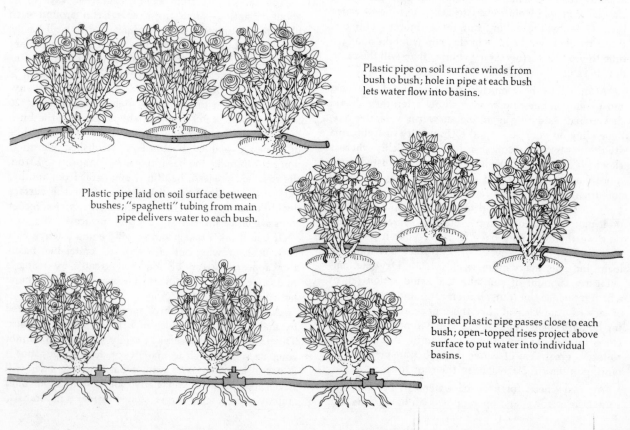

Plastic pipe on soil surface winds from bush to bush; hole in pipe at each bush lets water flow into basins.

Plastic pipe laid on soil surface between bushes; "spaghetti" tubing from main pipe delivers water to each bush.

Buried plastic pipe passes close to each bush; open-topped rises project above surface to put water into individual basins.

Any organic mulch will eventually decompose (some quickly, some over a period of years), and this process produces their final benefit. For in decomposing they constantly improve the structure of the upper soil zone, making it more open and therefore more receptive to water and air penetration and easier for the growth of surface feeder roots.

What Mulches to Use

Before you select a material for mulching, you need to know how that material acts when spread out in a layer and how fast it decomposes. The fast decomposing ones (manures, sawdust or wood shaving, compost, and lawn clippings, for example) will help improve the surface soil most quickly. But some of these—notably wood by-products (unless they are nitrogen fortified) —will take nitrogen from the soil to aid their decomposition; unless nitrogen is plentiful enough for both mulch and roses, your roses will suffer a deficiency. A *light* sprinkling of a high-nitrogen fertilizer should stave off any problem of competition for nitrogen. Manures, of course, are the classic example of a relatively quick-to-decompose material that contains enough nitrogen for its own breakdown.

Some materials, such as lawn clippings and some leaves, mat down so tightly that they prevent air and water from entering the soil. You can use lawn clippings, however, if you apply them in a thin layer and let that dry before adding fresh ones.

Cocoa bean hulls and other hard, crushed materials may be with you for several years but do the least toward improving soil structures. Rock mulches and ground covers absorb great amounts of heat and radiate it up underneath the foliage. This amounts to a hotfoot where summers are warm and dry.

Probably the trickiest material that could be used as a mulch—and therefore one to avoid—is peat moss. It dries out quickly after the original wetting and, if allowed to dry completely, becomes almost waterproof.

There are countless regionally available "waste" materials that you could use for mulching. In addition to manures and wood by-products, you might encounter crushed sugar cane residue (*bagasse*), cotton seed hulls, ground corn cobs, spent mushroom compost from mushroom farms, pine needles, or decomposed materials from the floor of forests or woods.

When applying any mulch, don't pile it up on the base of the canes; spread it to within about an inch of the base of each rose.

FERTILIZING

If a rose bush isn't fertilized, it won't necessarily wither away. In fact, many species and shrub roses can flourish reasonably well without any assistance from the plant pantry of nutrients. The public fancy, though, has fastened on the streamlined beauty of the hybrid tea or the opulence of a hybrid perpetual—not the simpler charm of the more self-sufficient wildlings—and these 20th century beauties *do* need fertilizer in order to dazzle us with bloom. Along with beautiful flowers and foliage, additional benefits come from a sensible fertilization program. A rose in vigorous good health is better able to withstand invasions of insects or diseases than is the one struggling for survival, and where winters are severe the plant that has been healthy all year is more likely than the weakling to cope successfully with winter cold.

What Are the Major Nutrients?

Like most familiar plants, roses require principally three nutrients for healthy growth: nitrogen, phosphorus, and potassium. All garden soils contain these nutrients in varied quantities. But because plants continually are at work diminishing the supply, sooner or later the gardener must begin to replenish the soil's reserves. The reasons for the importance of nutrients to roses are discussed in the following paragraphs.

• *Nitrogen* controls the rate and quantity of growth by regulating a plant's ability to make proteins, the growth promoters contained in each plant cell. When roses receive enough nitrogen, they produce an abundance of canes, stems, and leaves. If you apply too much, though, you simply overstimulate vegetative production at the expense of flowers, possibly ending up with lush foliage that lacks disease resistance and weak, spindly growth that can be damaged easily by cold. (Or, you may end up with a dead plant—a casualty of fertilizer-burned roots.) Roses that are just sitting still or are only half-heartedly performing may need the stimulating tonic of a nitrogenous fertilizer. No other nutrient so rapidly improves growth when properly applied (see page 25), as long as plants are receiving adequate water. Nitrogen's effects are shown quickly in an increased volume of growth, more intense green color, greater leaf size, and more and better blooms.

A gas in its elemental form, nitrogen is available to plants only from the compounds it forms with other elements and then it is usable largely in its nitrate form. (Nitrogen in its ammonia or nitrite forms usually is converted by soil microorganisms into nitrate to be used readily by plants.) Another peculiarity of nitrogen is that it is readily water soluble in most of its compounds. Unlike the other nutrients, nitrogen is not easy to stockpile in the soil because of this solubility. Much of the nitrogen not taken up by the rose soon after application will be leached out of the root zone by routine deep waterings and rain, especially in sandy soil.

• *Phosphorus* may be thought of as a regulator of the plant's seasonal life cycle. When soils contain enough available phosphorus compounds, root development begins early in the season, permitting early assimilation of other nutrients. Flower formation also is encouraged, for phosphorus plays a vital role in seed production and, later on, the maturity of the plant's growth. Plants need phosphorus for production of sugars, and it provides the mechanism by which energy released by the burning of these sugars is transferred within the plant. In definitely acid soils, phosphorus may be plentiful but will be in insoluble compounds; raising your soil's pH to the range suitable for roses (see page 25) will release much of this locked up reserve. When other nutrients are available, a phosphorus deficiency may show as stunted growth with fewer flowers than normal. Because so little phosphorus is lost through leaching, it is best applied at planting time in the soil at the bottom of the planting hole.

• *Potassium* is the third member of the vital trio. Like nitrogen and phosphorus it is not available to plants in its elemental form but always through the compound potassium pentoxide (K_2O), usually referred to as "potash." As an important "body builder" of plants, potassium contributes to the manufacture and movement of sugars, starches, and cellulose. It promotes the growth of strong canes and builds resistance to low temperatures.

You are less likely to encounter a potassium deficiency than a low level of nitrogen or phosphorus. Clay soils and the heavier loams generally contain enough; it is in lighter, sandier soils or in highly organic "peat" soils that potassium is most likely to be low.

LACK of available iron results in chlorosis: pale, yellow-green leaves, dark veins. Normal foliage is at right.

Secondary and Trace Nutrients

Only because plants need calcium, magnesium, and sulfur in far smaller amounts than they do the "big three" (nitrogen, phosphorus, and potassium), are these nutrients called "secondary." But, a short supply of any one of these second string nutrients can affect your roses as negatively as a lack of any of the main team.

Calcium helps in the manufacture and growth of plant cells and aids root system growth. Magnesium is an important component of chlorophyll, the green material in the leaves that is necessary for photosynthesis to take place. Sulfur, like nitrogen, contributes to the formation of plant proteins.

Seven other nutrients in the soil—boron, chlorine, copper, iron, manganese, molybdenum, and zinc—provide essential elements for proper plant development, but each is needed only in very small quantities. An iron deficiency called *chlorosis* probably is the most frequently encountered trace element lack: leaves turn yellow but veins remain green. Usually the problem stems from iron in the soil being unavailable to plants rather than from its being absent. This happens most often in alkaline soils.

Usually you will find no deficiency of any trace nutrients, except in situations of extreme soil acidity or alkalinity (see box on soil testing, next page). An adjustment of pH to a range favorable to roses may be all that is necessary to restore a trace element availability. Any addition of trace elements (other than iron) to your soil should be done with caution and preferably only after you have had your soil tested for pH and analyzed for nutrient content. An overabundance of these trace nutrients can be as detrimental as an under-supply.

Remember that *all* nutrients must be available to your roses for them to produce vigorous, healthy plants. A deficiency or absence of any one will show in the way your roses grow or in their leaves.

Fertilizer Types and How to Use Them

The choice is yours: whether to use a balanced fertilizer that contains the necessary nutrients or whether to apply the nutrients separately from different sources. What is important is that there be enough nutrients available in the soil solution to get your roses off to a good start and keep them going. In order for the roots to assimilate nutrients they must be in solution in the ground water which surrounds each soil particle. And, how these nutrients are supplied and how they get to the roots is important to every rose grower.

Basically, you can separate the fertilizers into two categories: organic and inorganic. Organic fertilizers are derived from once-living organisms—plants (compost or cottonseed meal, for example) or animals (such as manures, bone meal, or blood meal). In most cases you can count on the dry organics to be slower acting than dry inorganics because most of them must first be acted upon by soil microorganisms in order to release nutrients. (Manure is a notable exception, for its nitrogen is simply leached out by water).

Organic fertilizers offer several advantages. They all contribute, more or less, to the organic matter content of your soil, helping it to maintain a good structure. They are unlikely to stimulate your plants too early (or too late) in the year because the soil organisms that aid their conversion to useable nutrients are not active unless the soil is warm. You run less risk of applying too much fertilizer because nutrient concentrations are generally lower than those in inorganics and because organics require the intermediate step with microorganisms. A drawback to organics may be cost per pound of actual nutrient. Pound for pound, most organic fertilizers contain a smaller quantity of a given nutrient than do many inorganics. For example, you would need about a ton of manure to supply the amount of nitrogen available in a 25-pound bag of ammonium sulfate.

The advantage of the inorganic fertilizers is that they can supply a predictable amount and kinds of nutrients that are available without delay—and without any harm if used according to directions. If carelessly used, however, the application can do more harm than no dose at all: highly concentrated nutrient solutions reaching roots all at once may inflict considerable damage to young roots. And, of course, the gardener who relies solely upon inorganics for plant nutrition without adding or-

ganic materials to improve his *soil* is likely to find himself with a gradually deteriorated soil structure—and consequent poor plant growth.

In recent years two sorts of inorganic fertilizers have been developed to overcome some of the potential disadvantages of many inorganics. Urea (or urea-form, short for urea-formaldehyde) is a synthetically produced equivalent of the nitrogen in animal urine. Its nitrogen content is high, and so is its resistance to leaching. Inorganics also have been produced in various slow-release formulations, designed for a gradual, more lasting effect after application.

When selecting a fertilizer, remember that it should supply the necessary nutrients when the bushes need them. The first spring growth will be better served by an immediately available inorganic fertilizer in case soil microorganisms have not yet "awakened" for the year. Likewise, an early autumn application of soluble inorganic phosphorus-potash fertilizer will help to promote maturity and contribute to the plants' abilities to withstand winter cold where this is a problem. During the growing season, however, the choice is wide open. And to supplement soil fertilization, don't overlook liquid fertilizers for soil or leaves (see page 26).

Your Fertilizer Choices

Your roses can assimilate nutrients in two ways: through their roots and through their leaves. Spraying fertilizer solutions onto foliage can be a beneficial *supplement* to soil fertilization; see page 27 for a few guidelines for this method.

You can apply some of the major and secondary nutrients separately. But many rose growers, both new and the old hands, prefer the convenience of a good, balanced, dry commercial fertilizer. In these fertilizers the major nutrients (and sometimes the secondary ones) are blended in specific proportions, guaranteeing a uniform relationship between the nutrients. Some of these balanced fertilizers, marketed as "rose food," have nutrients in proportions that will suit most rose growing conditions throughout the country. For the new rose grower, this is the easiest sort of fertilizer to use. Some even contain systemic insecticides that remain effective for about a month in the plant and can kill sucking insects during that time.

Usually on the front of the packages of these "complete" fertilizers you will find three numbers, for example: 1–2–3. These numbers indicate the proportions of the three major nutrients, nitrogen, phosphorus, and potassium, in that order. (Translation: the fertilizer contains 1 per cent nitrogen, 2 per cent phosphoric acid, and 3 per cent potash.) These percentages will be listed, beginning with nitrogen, on the back of the package as will percentages of any other nutrients in the fertilizer.

With any of these fertilizers, *carefully* follow directions and dosage instructions on the package. Don't think that if a little fertilizer is good, more will be better: this can do more harm than good. If you are tempted to deviate from the recommendations, use *less* at a time but make the applications a little more often.

How and When To Fertilize

Before you apply dry commercial fertilizers, be sure the soil is moist to avoid burning roots. The simplest insurance is to water your roses the day before you plan to fertilize. On the next day, *lightly* scratch up the soil surface (no more than about ¹/₂-inch deep) and scatter the directed amount of fertilizer beneath the bush out to the edge of its foliage drip line, keeping it several inches away from the base of the plant. Then—and this is most important—thoroughly soak in the fertilizer.

Fertilize first in early spring soon after you finish pruning. But following this application, there are at least two schools of thought that differ about when to give bushes more fertilizer throughout the rest of the season.

One "school" says that fertilizers should be synchronized with blooming periods of your roses so that plants will receive the nutrients when they need them most: just after they have completed one burst of bloom and need to make new growth for the next. This has been called, by at least one eminent rosarian, the "pat-on-the-back" method of fertilization. If you want to break it down to numbers and enter it on the calendar, you can figure that on the average the cycle of growth from the start of a flowering shoot to the opening of a bud covers 45-60 days.

The second fertilization theory might be called the "kick-in-the-pants" method. Following this, you fertilize in smaller doses, but regularly: every two, three, or four weeks. Those who do it as often as two weeks

apart usually alternate a dry fertilizer with a liquid soil or foliar fertilizer (see below). This theory holds that a plant's nutrient need is continuous. Nitrogen, especially, may be so easily leached from the soil that one heavy application every six weeks may not continue to provide enough for a plant during that entire period.

Actually, both approaches can work very well. The "pat-on-the-back" method is easier simply because you fertilize less often; but if that is your choice, you will want to stick to the powdered or pelletized dry fertilizers that release their nutrients over a period of time. Gardeners with fast draining sandy soils usually find they get better overall performance from the more-frequent method.

Rose growers in regions where winter temperatures dip below about 10° have to consider when to *stop* fertilizing. Succulent new growth late in the season is likely to be ruined by fall frosts, and the plant that still is actively growing when freezing weather arrives is at a real disadvantage in getting through winter with little damage. Depending on how early the first damaging frost usually is expected, cold climate rosarians give their last nitrogen applications anywhere from August 1 to early September—or no later than six weeks before anticipated freezing. Among many rose growers in these regions it is common practice to apply a phosphorus and potash fertilizer (say, 0-20-20 formula) a month to six weeks before frosts arrive in order to stop growth and bring canes to maturity.

Liquid Fertilizers

Because they are so easy to apply and roots can absorb their nutrients so quickly, liquid fertilizers are

---

WHAT SUCKER GROWTH IS

Any growth on a budded rose bush that comes from below the point where the named variety was budded onto the understock (see page 30) is a sucker. And all that a sucker is, really, is the understock plant trying to grow its own leaves and stems. Because a number of different understocks are in general use, no specific identifying characteristics can guide you in recognizing sucker growth. But one point is certain: the growth will be different from the rose it supports—often a long, slender, flexible cane. If you planted your roses with bud unions above soil level, you easily can see if the growth in question comes from below. For roses with bud unions at or slightly below the soil surface, carefully dig down to the growth's point of origin. If you determine you have a sucker on your hands, sharply *pull* it down and off the plant. Merely cutting it off leaves undeveloped growth eyes at the sucker's base which will trouble you with more suckers in the future.

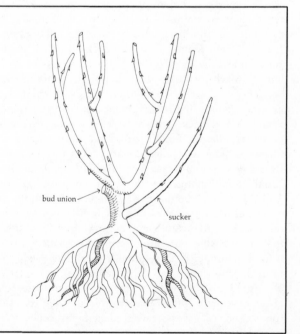

bud union

sucker

justifiably popular among many conscientious rose growers. Their nutrients are made available to the plant almost immediately, often resulting in a quick response you can almost see happening. Liquids are a great shot in the arm for neglected bushes and a fine supplement to dry fertilizers. You can select from an extensive array of brands and formulas, either organic or inorganic.

If you grow only a few bushes, you may be content to mix the solution in a watering can and go from bush to bush with it, mixing as many cansful as needed. However, for a large rose garden you'll probably want to make a small investment in a siphon hose attachment. With this you mix a bucketful of concentrated fertilizer solution. The water flowing through the hose extracts a measured amount of this fertilizer through the siphon and dilutes it to the proper strength in the water that comes out of the hose.

Foliar Fertilizing

To fertilize roses through their leaves is simple. Just spray the nutrient solution on the foliage as you would an insecticide. The nutrient solution is taken into the leaves through the breathing pores (stomates) on their undersides and is available almost immediately for the plant's use. Many foliar fertilizers can be mixed with some of the common insecticides and fungicides so that one trip around the garden can accomplish several objectives. But don't guess—be sure all are compatible. Check labels for any warnings, ask a Consulting Rosarian (see page 35), or check with the nearest state or county department of agriculture if there is any question.

Foliar fertilization is no miracle worker, but it can be a very helpful *supplement* to regular soil fertilizers, leading to these possible improvements in your roses: more strong canes originating from the lower portions of your bushes; larger and darker green leaves; more flowers.

Because more of the fertilizer is absorbed on the undersides of leaves, be sure you direct the spray there; upper surfaces will be covered by the "rain back" from this spray. Add a "spreader-sticker" to the solution to insure the spray's adhering to the leaves; or use a household dishwashing detergent for the same purpose, about 1/4 teaspoon to a gallon of solution, adding the detergent after the fertilizer solution has been mixed.

If you decide to try foliar fertilization, be sure to use a fertilizer that is made for the purpose and follow label directions exactly. Too concentrated a solution is almost sure to cause some leaf burn. A consistent program is best if you expect to reap the full rewards of this method. Begin in spring when the first leaves have formed and continue every two to three weeks until midsummer in cold-winter regions or until about mid-September where winters are mild. One word of caution: foliar fertilizing also may cause leaf burn in hot weather. As a rule-of-thumb, if temperatures are 90° or above, stop your foliar program and resume it when weather cools down.

GROWING ROSES IN CONTAINERS

Even though roses growing in five-gallon cans or the equivalent are a common sight in nurseries, surprisingly few gardeners think of roses as plants for container culture. And yet these same gardeners unhesitatingly plant other flowering shrubs in containers—shrubs such as camellias, rhododendrons, and azaleas—and carefully nurture them for the pleasure of their much briefer flowering seasons. Roses in containers are a possibility in any part of the country. Where winters are severe, their least attractive stage (dormancy) is shared by all other outdoor flowering plants, so the roses' appearance during these months puts them at no competitive disadvantage. Winter protection is simplified since plants can be moved without disturbing the roots to sheltered porches, garage, or basement—wherever temperatures can stay in the 15°-25° range. Where winters are mild but roses are semi-dormant at that season, you can move tubbed roses away from center stage and bring on the camellias, rhododendrons, and azaleas.

Before you decide that you're going to smother your patio or terrace with tubbed roses, realize that any container-grown plant is going to require more care than the same plant in the ground. Not that the care will be different; you just have to pay closer attention to the routine culture essentials. Watering in particular assumes increased importance. You simply cannot let

FERTILIZING won't help this problem: mosaic virus is a plant disease with no cure. Replace rose with new one.

tubbed roses dry out to the wilting point too often and expect even mediocre results. Because containers are exposed to the elements on all sides and have no direct contact with the soil, they dry out more rapidly than the ground does and have no sub-surface water reserves to draw upon beyond what is in the potting soil. You'll undoubtedly want to pay close—perhaps closer—attention to insect and disease control to keep foliage and flowers in the best possible condition. A rose to be viewed close-up loses all its value if its condition isn't worth looking at!

On the positive side, in some instances care of tubbed roses can be easier than care of rose garden plants, and often it will be better care because you can be more thorough. In watering, you'll know all roots have received their share when you see water draining out of the container. Spraying is easier and potentially more thorough because you can get at all sides of the tubbed plant. And fertilizing (especially liquid) goes on quickly and is directed entirely to the rose's root zone.

What Roses to Plant

Aside from good care, the type of rose you choose for container display has the greatest bearing upon your satisfaction. As a general rule, the floribundas, polyanthas, and miniatures are best adapted to container culture: their growth tends to be compact and bushy, of moderate height, and their habit is to flower almost continuously throughout the rose season. As a dividend, their cluster-flowering gives you a greater amount of bloom per flowering shoot than you will get from the larger but single-flowered hybrid teas. Virtually all grandifloras and the hybrid teas that have large or bulky bushes will be less satisfactory. They will grow well enough but quickly can become tall and topheavy, expanding entirely out of scale with their containers. Their flowering, too, usually is less frequent than that of floribundas and polyanthas. If you want to try some hybrid teas in containers, stick to the shorter or thin-caned sorts.

Containers, Soils, and Care

Square or rectangular, straight-sided wooden boxes are the best containers for roses because they offer more root room than pots or round, tapered tubs. These are sold at most nurseries, garden supply shops, or by mail order in a variety of kinds and sizes. If you're a handy carpenter you easily can make your own. Be sure planters are made from decay-resistant wood: redwood, cedar, or cypress. Don't skimp on the size of the container. A 14-inch square wooden box is about the smallest you'll want to use for polyanthas and smaller floribundas, while hybrid teas and the more robust floribundas will be better off in 16-20-inch boxes. For any container, about a 16-inch depth is minimum. Filled with damp soil, any of these containers will be quite heavy. If you plan to move them from place to place, you might want to attach casters to the container bot-

toms or put each container on a platform with casters. If you choose the latter, make sure the platform has drainage holes that line up with those in the container.

Of greatest importance in a container soil mixture is the soil's structure: this is what determines the air-water relationship discussed on page 12. Your tubbed roses will need a well-drained and non-compacting medium. This is most easily achieved by mixing your garden soil with organic materials, such as peat moss or any of the commercially packaged planting mixes. If your topsoil is on the heavy (clay) side, use a mixture of half garden soil to half organic material; for lighter soils, you can use a greater percentage of soil—about two parts to one of organic. And for each container, mix in about a 4-inch potful of bone meal.

After you cover the bottom of the container with prepared planting mixture, set the bare root plant inside. You may have to bend the roots slightly to fit into the container, but they shouldn't be so long that they have to coil around the bottom. If they are, cut off the part that coils. Center the plant, spread out the roots, and fill in around them with the prepared soil, firming it well with your fingers around the roots and under the crown. When you are finished planting, the bud union should be about 1 inch above the soil and the soil surface about 2 inches below the container's rim.

After firming the plant in, water it thoroughly so that water runs out the drainage holes, saturating all the soil in the container. If the soil settles too much, add more and water it in until it remains about 2 inches below the top of the container. If the rose bush has also settled, jiggle it from side to side while pulling upward on the shank between roots and bud union until it returns to its proper depth. Do this during the time that the planting soil is flooded so you won't tear or break roots.

After growth begins, water often enough to keep soil moist but not soggy; never let soil dry out to the point that the plant droops. In really hot weather, check your tubbed roses daily just to be safe. Otherwise, watering about every third day should be sufficient. Always give plants enough water so that it runs out the drainage holes; just moistening the soil surface will keep your roses constantly thirsty.

Because frequent and thorough watering continually leaches soluble nutrients from container soil mixtures, you'll want to fertilize regularly during the growing season. Liquid fertilizers are simple to mix and apply, are available immediately to the roses, and are the safest to use in containers since you can regulate the concentration in each application regardless of how much solution you apply. If you fertilize about every two weeks after growth begins you should have roses in lusty good health all season. Should you prefer to use a dry fertilizer, be sure you use one that is completely water soluble so that undissolved elements will not build up in the soil. Apply dry fertilizers evenly, scratching them lightly into the soil, then water thoroughly. Conservatively follow recommendations for how much to apply, and use it no more often than specified.

MINIATURE ROSES

The popularity of miniature roses derives from their overall daintiness: they are perfectly scaled-down replicas of modern floribundas or hybrid teas in all the colors of their larger kin. Some have produced climbing sports (or are natural climbers) and many are also available as miniature standards.

Miniatures have bushy plants 1 foot tall or less with wiry stems and narrow, closely set foliage. Recent hybridizing, in which larger modern roses have been used to increase the color range of miniatures, has produced some plants that may grow to about 1½ feet—especially if planted outdoors in the ground. These are still acceptable miniatures as long as flowers and plants are in proportion and retain the characteristic dainty appearance. But, a mixed planting of miniatures may not be uniform unless you select varieties having similar growth habits.

In contrast to nearly all other roses sold, bush and climbing miniatures should be grown on their own roots. Even normally small plants may grow too large if budded onto understocks, losing much of their diminutive charm. Another difference is that miniatures rarely are sold bare-root. Plants purchased locally will be in small pots, and mail-order plants usually will come in pots or with the root balls intact and wrapped in plastic or moist sphagnum moss. Leaves on mail-order plants may be yellowed or drooping upon arrival, but don't worry: just soak the entire plant overnight in water.

Miniatures outdoors. Their soil requirements (see pages 12-15) and need for sunshine are no different from other roses, but there is one important planting difference: set miniatures slightly lower than they were in their nursery containers (but not so deep that soil covers the base of lowest branches). This encourages more root formation. For mass effect, space plants a foot apart unless you live in a mild climate where plants tend to grow bulkier.

Root systems are extensive but rather shallow, so a temporary drought imposed by a neglectful gardener is much more critical to these plants than to their larger and more deep-rooted brethren. See that soil is always moist but not soggy. Almost certainly you'll want to use a mulch to help conserve moisture —and remember that a fine-textured mulch is more in keeping with the sizes of these roses.

Although miniatures are small, they still need fertilizers for best growth. Don't fertilize newly planted bushes; wait until they produce their first crop of bloom, then use a liquid fertilizer every 3-4 weeks during the rest of the season. If you live where winter protection is a must, make your last fertilizer application at the same time you would for your other garden roses (see page 26). In their second and subsequent years in your garden, give plants a dry complete fertilizer at the start of the growing season— about a tablespoonful per plant. Do avoid fertilizers that are very high in nitrogen: they will only stimulate excessive growth.

Pruning should consist of removing weak, twiggy wood and reducing the length of any extra-vigorous growth that upsets the symmetry of the plant. During the growing season, watch for any long, rank growth and pinch or cut it back to promote branching.

Miniatures in containers. For new bushes, a 6-inch pot is a good beginning; miniature standards may need an 8, 10, or 12-inch pot or tub at first. Any container will be suitable as long as it provides at least a 5-inch soil depth and has drainage holes. For a good, basic soil mixture, see page 28. Miniatures in containers require even closer attention to watering than do plants in the ground. Whenever you water them, be sure you give enough so that water drains out of the container; this ensures thorough watering and flushes out any potentially harmful salts that could accumulate in the potting soil.

Indoor culture. Temperature, humidity, and light are the three factors that most influence your success with miniatures indoors. Give plants full sunlight in a room that is 70-75° during the day and about 10 degrees cooler at night. Don't put the plants on a narrow window sill; the sun through the glass may burn them, and the night air will chill. The dry atmosphere of the average home is too arid for their liking. To provide more humidity around the plants, set them on trays of gravel and fill the tray with water up to the container's base. The evaporating water will provide a more outdoor atmosphere. Fluorescent lights—either regular type or those made especially for growing plants—can provide adequate light for miniatures indoors if you have no sunny window space. For best performance, suspend two tubes with a reflector 10-14 inches above the plants.

MINIATURE rose 'June Time'

THREE PROPAGATION METHODS

Every winter and early spring, nurseries bulge with sturdy bare-root rose bushes, and mail-order nurseries are ready to deliver equally husky plants at the drop of a letter. Why then, you might ask, should you bother to propagate roses when good plants are so available.

Various practical considerations aside, the chief reason for wanting to propagate your own roses is for the pleasure of it. Words can't quite capture the satisfaction provided by beautiful blooms on a rose bush that *you* nurtured from a scrap of wood. Of course, if you want more plants of a particular rose that no longer is sold or of one you can't identify, then you'll have to grow your own—either from cuttings or by budding onto understock plants. Should you want to try budding, you also have the chance to make a standard (or "tree") rose of any bush variety you choose. Or if you have the creative urge (and are somewhat of a gambler at heart), you can try raising entirely new roses from seed.

Budding

Virtually all rose bushes sold bare-root are budded plants. At the proper time of year, professional budders slice growth eyes or "buds" from stems of the roses they want to propagate and insert them into incisions in the bark on well-rooted cuttings of another rose known to give good root systems. There are several good reasons for propagating roses this way. Not all modern hybrids grow vigorously on their own roots, but when they have a strong root system under them, they will perform well. Some roses, regardless of how good or poor their own roots are, are very difficult to root and would always be in short supply if they had to be propagated by cuttings. To the commercial grower it means faster production of new varieties: a cutting long enough to be rooted will have at least four buds, but each of these buds inserted into understock could produce a separate plant. The commercial grower also needs plants which can be dug easily without damage to roots and which have roots that will pack and ship easily. Consequently, most commercial understocks have relatively flexible and not-too-thick roots which can be dug simply and will bend rather than break in packing.

Commercial growers who ship nationally also look for understocks that will grow well under the greatest possible variety of growing conditions. As yet, no perfect understock has been developed that is suitable for all regions, but two of the most widely adaptable are *Rosa multiflora,* a species from Japan, and the semi-double, maroon-red climber 'Dr. Huey.' Multiflora is preferred for cold-winter areas; 'Dr. Huey,' with a shorter dormancy requirement, is better for most of the southwest and other fairly mild-winter regions. Other mild-winter understocks are 'Odorata' (an old Chinese garden hybrid) and *Rosa fortuneana*—the latter good for the unusual Florida conditions where roses never go dormant and most soils are fast draining and nematode infested.

Perhaps the simplest understock source is sucker growth from any of the roses in your garden. If one got away from you during the previous year so that it grew long and matured its wood, you can cut it into eight-inch pieces and root them as described for hardwood cuttings on page 31. The only difference is that you'll want to gouge out all eyes on the cuttings except for the top two; any eyes left below the point where you would insert the bud are potential sucker sources. Cuttings that are pencil-thick or slightly larger (about $3/8$-$5/8$-inch diameter) are the easiest to bud.

Since your budding will be on a small scale and for your own amusement, you won't be so concerned with the commercial growers' need for flexible roots that dig and ship easily. All you need is something that roots easily and well and that will accept the majority of buds you put on it. Among the old rambler types, 'American Pillar,' 'Crimson Rambler,' 'Dorothy Perkins,' and 'Veilchenblau' have been successful. If you live in a mild-winter area, you might also try the Banksias and 'Climbing Cecile Brunner.'

Sometimes you can buy Multiflora plants for hedges or erosion control plantings. These plants may be suitable for budding the summer after you plant them; and just one, allowed to grow, will supply you with understock cuttings for years to come. Another rose occasionally sold for hedging (under the commercial synonym 'Red Robin') is the old hybrid China 'Gloire des Rosomanes.' Until 'Dr. Huey' came along, this was the most used understock for the drier, milder regions where it was known as 'Ragged Robin.'

Spring and summer are budding seasons; the earlier the growing season begins, the sooner you can bud. The understock must be succulent enough so that its bark will peel back easily from the woody core of the stem; take buds from a stem that has just finished flowering.

You need two "tools" for budding: a very sharp knife, and something to tie-in the bud when the operation is finished. You can buy special budding knives, which assure you of a good, sharp edge. Some of these are made with flattened handles designed to lift the flaps of bark formed by the T cut. Moistened raffia once was the standard tie for budding, but this has been replaced by rubber strips 5-8 inches long, known as "budding rubber." Even simpler to use—because they require no tying—are plastic bud coverings. These are clear plastic patches which you wrap completely over the bud and clip together on the opposite side of the stem from the bud. Both plastic and rubber budding wraps are sold by horticultural supply houses. A good local nursery or your county agricultural office should be able to suggest a source for them.

In three to four weeks, you should have evidence of your success or failure. Cut the wrapping and look at the bud you inserted: if it is plump and green, you're on your way to a new rose bush. If, instead, it is black and shriveled, don't despair; try another bud on the opposite side of the same understock and just a little lower down than the original.

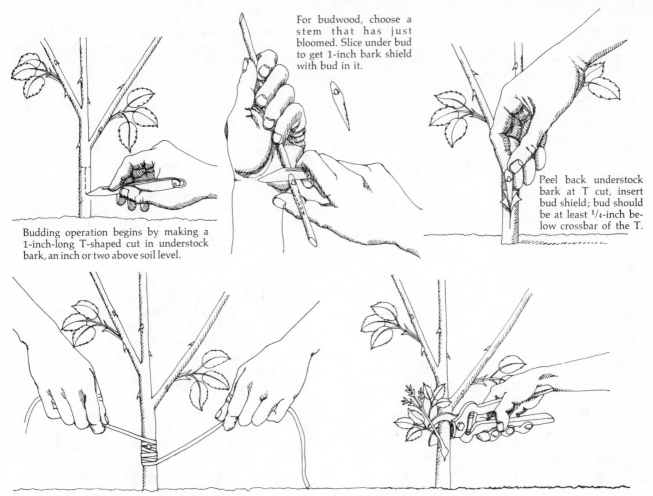

For budwood, choose a stem that has just bloomed. Slice under bud to get 1-inch bark shield with bud in it.

Budding operation begins by making a 1-inch-long T-shaped cut in understock bark, an inch or two above soil level.

Peel back understock bark at T cut, insert bud shield; bud should be at least 1/4-inch below crossbar of the T.

Firmly tie bud in place, wrapping both above and below it but leaving bud exposed.

When the bud sends out a strong new shoot next spring, cut off understock growth about 1 inch above it.

NEW PLANTS FROM CUTTINGS

Propagation by cuttings is the simplest way to grow additional plants of a favorite rose: you need no special skills or equipment. The most satisfactory "own-root" roses usually are the teas, hybrid perpetuals, and various shrub and old roses which are naturally very vigorous. Many hybrid teas are not as satisfactory when grown from cuttings as they are when budded onto an understock; take cuttings from the strongest growing hybrid teas if you want the best chances of success. In most cases, any cutting grown rose won't begin to make much of an impression in your garden until its third year, at which point it is the same age as the newly planted two-year-old bare root bush.

You can start cuttings from dormant wood at pruning time or take softwood cuttings during the blooming season. For dormant cuttings, select pencil-diameter wood and make the cuttings about 8 inches long. Remove the lowest two eyes, dip the end to be rooted in a rooting hormone powder (sold at most nurseries), and insert 2-3 inches deep in a pot or in the ground. If you plant directly in the ground, make a trench in the soil, put 1/2-1 inch of coarse sand in the bottom, and fill in around the cuttings with a half-and-half sand and soil mixture. Firm the soil and water the cuttings. For starting in pots, a light, sandy potting soil is the best. Either way, start the cuttings in a spot which receives little or no direct sunlight.

During the flowering season, you can start softwood cuttings from stems that just have bloomed. Cut off the faded flower just above the first five-leaflet leaf and make the second cut about six inches farther down the stem just below a leaf. You want at least four growth eyes on the cutting. Cut off all but the top two sets of leaves, dip the cuttings in a rooting hormone, then plant them in a sandy potting soil as described for dormant cuttings. Finally, water them in, cover the pot with a plastic bag or invert a glass jar over the cuttings, and place the pot somewhere out of direct sunlight. In a month or two, when new growth appears, you can remove the bag or jar. If you enclosed the entire pot in a plastic bag, you shouldn't need to give the cuttings any additional water during their rooting period. But if a glass jar is covering them, check often to be sure the soil doesn't dry out.

How to Hybridize

The mechanics of hybridizing are so simple that insects, the wind, and the roses themselves do it with the greatest of ease and frequency. The hips that decorate many old roses in autumn or that you try to remove from your hybrid teas are the result of such natural forces at work.

At first you may want to plant seeds from hips that form naturally. Until the mid 19th century most new roses came from such unplanned crosses. Doing this will give you the experience of harvesting, planting, and raising new plants with the minimum of disappointment should any fatalities occur. The blooms on these seedlings are likely to spur you on to planning and making definite crosses—either because they are so fascinating or because they are so nondescript that you feel a little guidance is needed!

In all regions where you can count on frosts in October, do all your hybridizing with the first crop of bloom in spring. Hips require about four months to form, mature, and ripen, and you want this process completed by the time cold weather arrives.

When mature hips turn orange, yellow, or brown, they are ready for picking. Usually this is in early autumn. In regions where the growing season is short, some rose hybridizers cover the full-sized hips in midsummer with aluminum foil. This hastens ripening so that all hips will be ready by the end of the season.

An after-ripening period of low (but not freezing) temperatures combined with moisture improves the percentage of germination. As you pick the ripe hips, put them in boxes or plastic bags where you can cover them with damp sand, vermiculite, or peat moss. Then, if you have room there, put these in the vegetable crisper of your refrigerator. You can leave the after-ripening hips outdoors if you prefer, but see to it that they are safe from mice and squirrels.

Any time from the beginning of December to mid-January, remove the hips from their after-ripening quarters (they'll be black and partly decomposed by then) and shell out the seeds. These will be of odd sizes and shapes, but a convenient indicator of which are good and which aren't is the water test: plant those which sink in water, discard seeds that float.

Growers of rose seedlings have many favorite ways to plant and germinate the seeds, but they break down to two basic methods: either you plant the seeds close together in fairly shallow containers and transplant seedlings soon after they come up or you sow them in flats or boxes where they will remain until they flower. The first method probably is more popular because, initially, it uses less space and less potting soil. But it does require more labor because you have to transplant. If you plant seeds where they are to bloom, use a flat or box at least 3 inches deep, sowing the seeds an inch apart in rows about two inches from one another. In either case, cover seeds with $3/8$-$1/2$ inch of the potting soil.

Seeds often will start to germinate within six weeks of planting and will continue for about two months. The first two leaves to appear are oval shaped and not at all rose-like; it is the second set that proves they are roses. As soon as this second set is out, you can transplant the seedlings. As an improvised trowel to lift the tiny plants, use something like a nail file, knife, or ice

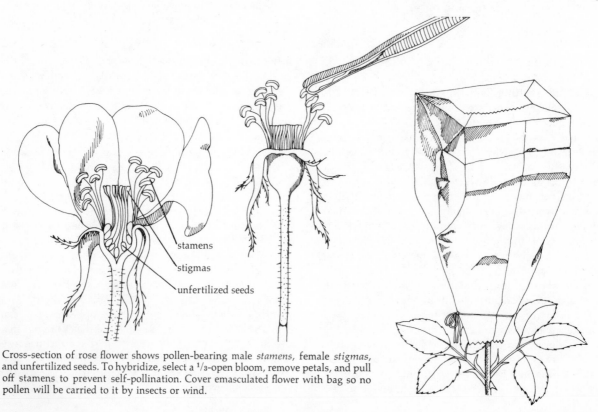

Cross-section of rose flower shows pollen-bearing male *stamens*, female *stigmas*, and unfertilized seeds. To hybridize, select a $1/3$-open bloom, remove petals, and pull off stamens to prevent self-pollination. Cover emasculated flower with bag so no pollen will be carried to it by insects or wind.

cream stick; try to keep some soil around their roots during the operation. If it is a cross you particularly value, you may want to keep the seed bed intact for another year. Some seeds which fail to germinate the first spring may grow the next year.

Growing the Seedlings

Here again—just as with seed planting—you have a choice of two basic ways to handle the seedlings: indoors or outside. Traditionally, rose seedlings would unfurl their first blooms in greenhouses, but this was done mostly to beat the often miserable spring weather in England and parts of France where so much hybridizing was (and still is) going on. A greenhouse still is quite satisfactory but by no means necessary. You can just as easily flower seedlings indoors in a sunny window or under artificial light.

Any of these indoor methods are most popular with hybridizers living where long and cold winters make the growing season short. A bush hybrid tea seedling may bloom as early as six weeks from germination (climbers and old rose seedlings take two to three years), so cold-climate gardeners can flower rose seedlings during winter and early spring before roses outside even have new growth. This gives seedlings the advantage of a long growing season the first year. During this period, the hybridizer has a chance to evaluate new plants early, then again on second and even third bloomings before the season is over. As soon as spring frost danger is past, you can move your seedlings outside. Protect them from wind and direct sunlight for about a week until they adjust to the outdoor atmosphere. If you wish to try them under artificial lights, use the 40-watt fluorescent tubes made especially for growing indoor plants. A two-tube fixture is satisfactory, a four-tube one even more so because of better light distribution. Arrange it so that the lights are about six inches above the containers in which the seedlings are growing. Leave the lights on for 16 hours each day.

Where winters are relatively mild—as in many parts of the South, Southwest, and West—there's not as much to be gained by flowering the seedlings indoors. Here, if you wish, you can prepare your seed beds outside. Just a raised bed with light, fast-draining soil could do for both germination and first flowering, although to save space you might want to germinate in flats of pots and transplant to the raised beds.

Damping off—a fungus which rots young seedlings at soil level—can plague seedlings of almost any plant. This is the reason for using sterilized soil and clean containers. As an added precaution, you may want to dust the seeds with captan before planting. Should any seedlings damp off, water the seed flats or pots with a Dexon solution or dust with captan. Mildew may bother seedlings, especially those grown outdoors; a dusting of sulfur should keep it in check.

Any seedlings you select may make fairly thrifty plants by their second or third year in your garden. But the only way you will be able to compare them fairly with commercially produced roses is to bud your seedlings onto one of the standard commercial understocks (see page 30). Sometimes you will notice improved blooms on your budded plants; almost always you will get a larger, more vigorous bush.

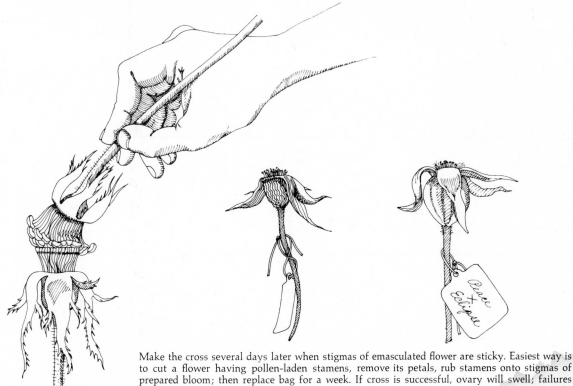

Make the cross several days later when stigmas of emasculated flower are sticky. Easiest way is to cut a flower having pollen-laden stamens, remove its petals, rub stamens onto stigmas of prepared bloom; then replace bag for a week. If cross is successful, ovary will swell; failures turn brown and shrivel. Tag each cross listing, seed parent first.

Fragrant Cloud

A Shopper's List of Favorite Varieties

Since color is the primary factor in most people's choices of roses, the descriptions and photographs through page 63 are arranged in color groups to give you a comparative idea of varieties of similar color. Within each category are grouped modern roses of various types: hybrid tea (HT), grandiflora (GR), floribunda (F), polyantha (P), and climber (CL). Where a bush rose also is available in climbing form, the code "CL" appears just beneath the variety's type in that column. Shrub and old garden roses—usually chosen for specific landscape use or for sentiment—appear on pages 61-63. It is impractical to give absolute heights for the roses described, for these depend upon climate, pruning, and general culture. But the relative sizes of low (L), medium (M), and tall (T) should hold in all regions: the tallest varieties in Midwestern and Eastern gardens also will be the tallest ones in frost-free areas of the West and South.

One of the greatest aids to selection is seeing roses growing in your area. Many municipalities have public rose gardens or at least public parks that feature a good assortment of roses. In addition, many local and regional rose societies hold spring and fall shows that usually are publicized in newspapers.

Recognizing the need for general information at the local level, The American Rose Society (4048 Roselea Place, Columbus, Ohio 43214) established the Consulting Rosarian program—a countrywide network of dedicated and experienced rose growers who have volunteered to give advice pertinent to their areas. The system was begun as a help to fledgling members of The American Rose Society; but—time permitting—these people also can advise serious non-members. Furthermore, they may be able to put you in touch with a nearby rose society, through which you could expand your fund of rose lore in the fellowship of other keen rose growers.

The abbreviation AARS designates an All-America Rose Selection. In carefully supervised test gardens throughout the country, forthcoming introductions may be grown and evaluated over a two-year period. Those that score high on all points of performance win the coveted AARS award. Since the first awards in 1940, this generally has been an indication of roses that will be satisfactory in nearly all parts of the country.

The bare-root bushes you buy in winter or early spring will have begun growth two years earlier as understock cuttings or seedlings. Budded during spring or summer, the canes you receive will be 1-1½ years old. These plants need a year to become established in your garden before they can produce typical growth or bloom. So for the first year, resist cutting flowers with stems and leaves (see page 70); in the years to follow, you can enjoy cut blooms indoors. For long-lasting cut roses, pick flowers in early morning or late afternoon, re-cut the stems under water, then plunge them into water up to the bases of the blooms. Leave all foliage on the stems: it absorbs water, too. Keep the blooms in a cool place overnight (if afternoon-picked) or for several hours (if cut in the morning), then arrange them. Roses held overnight from afternoon picking should be cut in tighter bud than you want in your arrangement; they will fill out and expand during the night.

Frensham

Christian Dior

Dortmund   Mister Lincoln

Chrysler Imperial

Kassel   *Europeana*

RED ROSES

Name	Color	Type	Height	Description
AMERICANA	Crimson red	HT	M	Its good, high-centered form and profusion of bloom mark it as an ideal cut-flower variety. Color is rich, medium red noteworthy for its lack of fading or bluing. Good fragrance.
AZTEC	Scarlet orange	HT	M	Huge, flawlessly formed flowers are a vibrant unfading color between orange and scarlet. Shiny, bright green leaves clothe a strong growing but spreading plant. Long lasting when cut; mild fragrance.
BLAZE	Scarlet	CL		Clusters of 2–3–inch, double flowers smother the plants over a long spring season, then continue in smaller bursts through summer and fall. Slight fragrance. Tough and trouble-free.
CARROUSEL	Vivid dark red	GR	T	Dark maroon red buds open to warm dark red blooms, some singly but more often in small clusters. Great for hedges or backgrounds: plants are vigorous, tall, and bushy.
CHRISTIAN DIOR	Cherry red	HT	T	AARS 1962. Elegant, blood red buds unfurl to slightly lighter red flowers that retain their attractiveness when fully open, do not fade or blue. Outside of petals is a little lighter and duller than inside. No fragrance.
CHRYSLER IMPERIAL	Dark crimson	HT CL	M	AARS 1953. Classic, velvety dark red with shapely buds, full flowers, and rich fragrance. Free flowering, bushy plants have dark green, rather dull foliage. A standard of comparison among reds.
CITY OF BELFAST	Orange scarlet	F	L	Brilliant blooms of orange-tinted scarlet—the same color as in 'Sarabande' but these are double and rosette shaped. Very free flowering on bushy, very disease resistant plants.
COMANCHE	Brick red	GR	M	AARS 1969. Large, perfectly shaped brick red flowers come singly as often as they do in small clusters. Large red-tinted leaves on a slightly spreading bush. Free flowering.
CRIMSON GLORY	Dark crimson	HT CL	L	Until 'Chrysler Imperial' arrived, this was THE red rose: lovely buds and full, velvety flowers with powerful fragrance. Low, vigorous, spreading plants. Not best in cool climates.
DON JUAN	Deep crimson	CL		A pillar-climber with 8–10 foot canes growing straight up. Deep, velvety red buds are of best hybrid tea form and size, come singly or in small clusters on long stems, and open well in all climates.
DORTMUND	Cherry red	CL		A Kordesii climber that also can be a ground cover or shrub. Beautiful, glossy, holly-like foliage. Three-inch flowers are single, bright cherry red with white centers, in large clusters.
EL CID	Red orange	HT	M	A fine splash of color for the garden. Medium sized glowing red-orange flowers are produced in quantity on a vigorous, bushy, somewhat spreading plant.
ENA HARKNESS	Bright red	HT	M	Long considered the best red for cool and foggy climates where many reds are dull or fail to open well. Long pointed buds and bright crimson open flowers; upright plant. Outclassed in hot country.
ERNEST H. MORSE	Currant red	HT	T	Another good wet-weather red. Plenty of large leathery dark green foliage to set off the large, perfectly formed, bright currant red blooms. Flowers are slow to open.
ETOILE DE HOLLANDE	Dark crimson	HT CL	M	In its second half-century now but still a fine rich red in all climates. Lovely high-centered buds open to heavily fragrant, unfading blooms on long stems. Vigorous, upright bushes.
EUROPEANA	Ruby red	F	L	AARS 1968. Low, spreading, strong growing bushes produce very large clusters of bright but deep red blooms. Individual flowers are to 3 inches across, full and rosette shaped.

Scarlet Knight   Sarabande

Oklahoma

Olé

ROSE VARIETIES   39

Name	Color	Type	Height	Description
FLORADORA	Scarlet orange	F	M	AARS 1945. The first orange-scarlet to be introduced. Strong, upright plants are clothed in bronzy green, glossy foliage. From globular buds come 2-inch cupped, double blooms in sprays of 6–12.
FRAGRANT CLOUD	Orange red	HT	M	Long scarlet-orange buds unfold to coral red, 30-petalled blooms that exude a delightfully intense fragrance; some come singly, others in small clusters. Bush is husky and trouble-free with lustrous foliage.
FRENSHAM	Dark crimson	F	T	Velvety red buds of best hybrid tea form open to semi-double unfading blooms with showy golden stamens. Tall, vigorous, vase-shaped, thorny bushes are excellent for hedges, background plants or shrubs. Glossy foliage.
GARNETTE	Dark crimson	F	L	A familiar florist rose, the very double, rosette-shaped blooms last a week to ten days indoors. Open flowers never lose their attractiveness. Holly-like foliage is susceptible to mildew.
GRAND SLAM	Cherry red	HT	M	A large, bushy plant produces quantities of well-formed, bright cherry red buds that hold their color without fading or bluing in the open flower. Mildly fragrant.
GYPSY	Orange red	HT	T	AARS 1973. Flashing ember red flowers and nearly black-red buds are flaunted on vigorous, medium-tall bushes. The healthy foliage is dark bronzy green.
JAZZ FEST	Cerise	F	M	Perfect hybrid tea refinement in a semi-double floribunda flower. Some blooms come singly but most are in clusters. The vigorous bush is somewhat spreading, about 2½ feet tall.
JOHN S. ARMSTRONG	Dark red	GR	T	AARS 1962. A dark, vibrant red that refuses to turn blue as it ages. Fairly short black-red buds open to many-petalled medium sized flowers, singly or in clusters, that last many days cut or on the bush.
KARL HERBST	Dark scarlet	HT	M	Sometimes called the "red Peace," as its husky plant and full flowers are reminiscent of its parent. The dark scarlet petals are lighter on the outside, and blooms open best in dry, warm weather.
KASSEL	Orange-scarlet	CL		Easily a climber in mild regions but can be used as a shrub anywhere; canes are long and arching. Flowers of hybrid tea size and shape come in small clusters: scarlet-orange buds, coral red open blooms.
KING OF HEARTS	Bright crimson	HT	M	Perfection of form in a medium sized bright crimson, good in all climates. Bushy, rather spreading, and thorny plants carry leathery, dark green foliage.
LILLI MARLENE	Dark red	F	M	Jaunty deep scarlet blooms are semi-double, to 3 inches across. Superb for mass plantings: growth is strong, compact, and regular, while clusters of flowers come continuously
LOTTE GUNTHART	Bright crimson	HT	T	An unmistakable flower, best when half to fully open. As many as 100 ruffled petals in each bloom create the appearance of a velvety red, 6-inch carnation. Plants are tall and bushy.
MIRANDY	Dark red	HT	M	AARS 1945. Outstanding in warm, humid regions, but blooms tend to ball and turn purple where it's cool and foggy. Intensely fragrant, well formed, full flowers; very bushy plant.
MISTER LINCOLN	Rich red	HT	T	AARS 1965. A completely satisfactory red for all regions: lovely long buds and full, fragrant open flowers. An easy growing, tall plant with long stems and dark glossy foliage.
NOCTURNE	Dark red	HT	M	AARS 1948. Another very dark red better in the Midwest, East, and South where summers are humid and warm. Longer slimmer buds and not so full a flower as its sister 'Mirandy.' Husky, bushy plant.

Name	Color	Type	Height	Description
OKLAHOMA	Black red	HT	T	The blackest buds imaginable open to very large, rather globular, dusky red blooms that still are beautiful when fully open. Heavy fragrance, lusty grower. Not at its best in cool, foggy areas.
OLD SMOOTHIE	Rich red	HT	T	Remarkable in that it is nearly thornless: some stems are, while others have just a few. Large, rich red, high-centered blooms come on vigorous, upright plants with medium green foliage.
OLÉ	Orange red	GR	M	An individual flower could be mistaken for a tuberous begonia or a carnation. Very double, ruffled and frilled blooms are a blinding red-orange. Very heavy blooming, bushy plants with holly-like leaves.
PAPA MEILLAND	Dark red	HT	M	Elegance in dark velvety crimson. Long, pointed buds open slowly to very fragrant double blooms—even in cool, damp weather, although foliage may mildew then. Upright plant.
PAUL'S SCARLET CLIMBER	Bright red	CL		A famous and widely planted cluster-flowering double red with one long and very profuse spring flowering season. Brilliant color is unfading. Vigorous growth to about 10 feet; hardier than hybrid tea climbers.
PHARAOH	Bright red	HT	T	Unfading, glowing red flowers develop from dark, velvety buds. Open blooms are cup shaped, with a black infusion on petal edges. Upright, bushy plants carry leathery, dark foliage.
RED CHIEF	Light, bright red	HT	T	Notably fragrant glowing light red with classically formed buds and attractive open flowers. Petals may burn in very hot weather. Plants are strong and upright with plenty of medium green leaves.
RED DEVIL	Bright, light red	HT	M	Flame red petals have a lighter, almost silvery reverse. Long, lovely buds on long stems open to full, symmetrical flowers that hold their color. Handsome glossy foliage, upright plant.
RED RADIANCE	Cerise red	HT	T	For over half a century a standard of dependability among light red roses. Flowers have an "old-fashioned" look—globular buds and cupped, very double blooms. Very vigorous and trouble free.
SAN ANTONIO	Deep red	GR	T	Heavy flower production and sunfast color are two of its outstanding assets. Medium length buds and very double flowers often come just one to a stem. Tall, strong, bushy plant with plenty of foliage.
SARABANDE	Oriental red	F	L	AARS 1960. Cheerful flowers are especially brilliant and have clusters of decorative stamens in their centers. Spreading plants are almost always in bloom, ideal for borders or foreground plantings.
SCARLET KNIGHT	Velvety scarlet	GR	M	AARS 1968. Plump black-red buds in small clusters unfurl to bright velvety red, thick petalled blooms about 5 inches across. Bushy, thorny, and vigorous, with dark bronze-green leaves. Fragrant.
SIMON BOLIVAR	Orange red	HT	M	Flashy orange-red flowers have a neon brilliance, frequently come in grandiflora-like clusters. Plenty of healthy, glossy, medium green foliage clothes a spreading, husky bush.
TAMANGO	Rose red	F	M	Hybrid tea-like buds and flowers usually come in small clusters, sometimes one to a stem. Color neither fades nor blues. The fast growing, bushy plants boast plenty of glossy, healthy foliage.
VALENTINE	Medium red	F	L	The brightest of bright red, fluffy 2-inch flowers almost cover the plants in their profusion. Bushes are no more than 2 feet tall and spreading—good for borders or foreground plantings.

Camelot

Duet

First Love

Bewitched

Charlotte Armstrong

PINK ROSES

Name	Color	Type	Height	Description
APRICOT NECTAR	Creamy apricot	F	M	AARS 1966. Large flower clusters are loaded with luscious creamy apricot hybrid tea-like blooms, each of which may be up to 4 inches across. Healthy, vigorous, and prolific bushes.
AQUARIUS	Deep rose	GR	T	AARS 1971. The cool rose-pink petals are overlaid deeper pink toward the margins. Long, beautifully tapered buds are produced in quantity, many of them one to a stem. Very vigorous, slender bushes.
BETTY PRIOR	Shrimp pink	F	T	All the charm of wild roses and much of the vigor, too. Red buds open to single, shell pink blooms that resemble dogwoods in size and shape. Strong growing, spreading bush with lots of bloom.
BEWITCHED	Rose pink	HT	T	AARS 1967. Stylish, long pointed buds with lighter reverse open slowly to fragrant, "show rose"-type flowers on long, strong stems. Healthy grayed green foliage clothes the vigorous, compact plants.
CAMELOT	Coral pink	GR	T	AARS 1965. The 5-inch, cup-shaped flowers open from rounded buds that nearly always come in clusters. Productivity and general health are its strong points; plants are vigorous with large, dark foliage.
CARLA	Light pink	HT	M	An undertone of salmon produces a noticeably warm pink color. Long, tapered buds open into large and long-lasting blossoms. Upright plants carry bronze-tinted foliage.
CECILE BRUNNER	Light pink	P CL	M	The bush may grow to only medium size, but watch out for the climber—it's rampant. Perfect miniature replicas of hybrid tea flowers come continuously throughout the year in graceful, thin-stemmed clusters.
CENTURY TWO	Dark rose	HT	M	This has the "ideal" rose buds: large, long, full-petalled, and fragrant. The outside of the petals is slightly deeper than the face. Husky plants are upright, bushy, with healthy foliage.
CHARLOTTE ARMSTRONG	Deep red-pink	HT CL	T	AARS 1941. The parent of countless stylish roses produced since its introduction. Famous for its long, elegantly slim buds that open to large, full flowers. Strong, bushy plant.
COMTESSE VANDAL	Coppery salmon	HT	L	An old favorite that still is treasured for the sculptured perfection of its buds. Two-toned bronze-pink buds open to large flowers that combine carmine, pink, buff, and gold. Watch for mildew.
CONFIDENCE	Pink and cream blend	HT	M	A large, full flower that needs warm weather to open properly. Well formed buds and open blooms combine pastel shades of pink, peach, and yellow with a distinct fragrance. Upright and bushy.
DAINTY BESS	Rose pink	HT CL	M	Graceful, perfect, 5-petalled single blossoms are a delicate pink with contrasting maroon-red anthers in the flowers' centers. Most of the 3–4 inch blooms come in clusters on the upright bushes.
DAY DREAM	Warm pink	HT	T	Big, bushy plants produce quantities of 5–6-inch flowers on long, strong cutting stems. The tapered buds and full open blooms are deep pink touched gold and are sweetly fragrant.
DUET	Dusky pink	HT	M	AARS 1961. A terrific flower producer with a cast-iron constitution. Medium sized buds and blooms are a two-toned dusky pink, darker on the outside of petals, and very long lasting. Holly-like leaves.
ELECTRON	Deep rose	HT	M	AARS 1973. Full, glowing rose pink blossoms slowly unfold from pointed buds; the regularly formed open flowers retain their attractiveness. Bushy plant with dark green foliage.

Royal Highness   *Showtime*

Miss All-American Beauty   *Rosenelfe*

Michele Meilland (top)
First Prize (center left)
Queen Elizabeth (lower left)
Tiffany (below)

Name	Color	Type	Height	Description
ELIZABETH OF GLAMIS	Coral salmon	F	M	Pronounce it "glahms." On the borderline between floribunda and hybrid tea, the 4-inch flowers open from well formed, pointed buds. Color deepens to almost orange in fall. Vigorous and upright.
FASHION	Coral	F	L	AARS 1950. The first of the coral-colored floribundas and still an exquisite flower. Ovoid buds in small clusters open to rather cupped 3-inch blooms. Bushy, spreading plant has bronzy foliage.
FIRST LOVE	Pearly pink	HT	T	It would be hard to imagine a longer, more slender and graceful bud than this rose has. In addition, the plant is tall and slender with elongated leaflets. Free blooming and a favorite for cutting.
FIRST PRIZE	Rich pink	HT	L	AARS 1970. Fabulous, very long, spiral buds of a deep pink unfold to really large flowers that are distinctly lighter in the center. Vigorous, spreading bushes are somewhat susceptible to mildew.
GENE BOERNER	Rose pink	F	M	AARS 1969. In every detail, the buds and flowers are perfect scaled-down models of the best hybrid teas. The clear, rose-pink blooms come both singly and in clusters on strong, upright bushes.
HELEN TRAUBEL	Salmon	HT	T	AARS 1952. Big, billowing bushes take up more space than many other roses but are well worth it. Great quantities of long pointed buds open quickly to large, rather loose flowers on flexible stems.
LITTLE DARLING	Pink and cream	F	T	Darling, but not little. Long, arching canes make this more of a shrub than a typical floribunda. Each pink and cream flower is perfectly formed and long lasting. Vigorous, trouble free.
MEMORIAM	Blush pink	HT	M	The more the buds unfurl, the more beautiful the flower becomes. Pastel pink to almost white, the blooms are quite freely produced for such a large flower. Vigorous, spreading, not for fogbound areas.
MICHELE MEILLAND	Creamy pink	HT	M	Only medium sized, but the rate of production is rapid and nearly each bloom is perfect. Color varies from creamy pink to creamy amber. Wiry stems good for cutting on a vigorous, bushy plant.
MISCHIEF	Salmon	HT	M	Another medium sized, consistently well-formed variety, but this time in a deep salmon color. And again the smaller size is compensated for in heavy bloom production. Compact, vigorous bushes.
MISS ALL-AMERI-CAN BEAUTY	Cerise pink	HT	M	AARS 1968. A big, bold blossom in a color you can't miss: something between a deep "shocking" pink and light red. Ovoid buds and well formed open flowers come on leathery-leaved, very husky plants.
NEW DAWN	Pale pink	CL		The first plant ever to be patented, and the first really cold-tolerant climbing rose having hybrid tea-like blooms. Flowers come in small clusters. Can be used also as a pillar type or bank cover.
PICTURE	Pink and salmon	HT CL	L	A time-honored favorite bearing "picture perfect" buds and blooms in several profuse bursts throughout the flowering season. The medium sized flowers are reminiscent of pink camellias. Bushy.
PINK FAVORITE	Rose pink	HT	M	This variety boasts some of the most beautiful foliage known among roses: shiny green, large and leathery. Large, well formed buds open quickly. Very vigorous, healthy.
PINK PEACE	Deep rose	HT	T	Not really a pink duplicate of 'Peace,' but it is a large, full and shapely, intense deep pink with heavy fragrance. Free flowering, very vigorous and upright bushes, but especially prone to rust.

Mojave   *Margo Koster*

Granada

Helen Traubel

Chicago Peace

Name	Color	Type	Height	Description
PORTRAIT	Creamy rose pink	HT	T	AARS 1972. A great rate of blossom production and an overall appearance of robust good health mark this as an excellent rose. Good sized, shapely buds open to 50-petalled flowers of rich pink shaded cream.
QUEEN ELIZABETH	Clear pink	GR CL	T	AARS 1955. For all practical purposes, a shrub rose— suitable for hedges and background plantings. Radiant pink, medium sized blooms develop from compact, pointed buds in small clusters. Extremely vigorous, tall, bulky bushes.
RADIANCE	Rose pink	HT CL	T	An "old-fashioned" appearing rose that for over half a century has been the example for good performance even when neglected. Ovoid buds open to double, cupped, two-toned blooms. Rugged bush.
RHONDA	Coral pink	CL		One that can be used as a pillar type, as well as fanned out horizontally for a restrained climber. Globular buds in small clusters open to medium sized blooms.
ROSE GAUJARD	Raspberry and white	HT	T	A beautiful bicolor of white and raspberry-rose, the white base color is brushed with pink to leave only the centers and bases of petals white. Very shapely, large blooms on an easy-to-grow bush.
ROSENELFE	Rose pink	F	M	Perfect, regular, camellia-like blooms of pure pink are carried in small clusters, each flower about 3 inches across. Healthy, vigorous plants are upright with attractive dark green foliage.
ROYAL HIGHNESS	Blush pink	HT	T	AARS 1963. Porcelain-like blush pink buds and flowers are of the highest quality. Long pointed buds, one to a stem, slowly unfold to magnificent full open blooms. Upright bushes.
SHOW GIRL	Deep carmine	HT CL	T	Deep rose pink with a blue cast to it, the artfully formed, very long buds open to equally large, fairly double blooms. At its best in spring and fall, and out of the fog belt. Upright.
SHOWTIME	Warm rose pink	HT	M	Somewhat ovoid, very shapely long buds come singly on strong stems; moderately double open flowers are fragrant. Bright green leaves cover the vigorous, bushy plants.
SOUTH SEAS	Coral salmon	HT	T	Really large but gracefully ruffled open flowers develop from slow opening buds of a deep shell pink. Notably vigorous, slightly spreading bushes have bronze-tinted foliage.
SUNRISE-SUNSET	Pink and cream	HT	M	A distinctive mingling of soft pink and cream, sometimes with tinges of tannish lavender at the base of petals. Attractive long buds open to light-centered blossoms.
SUNSET JUBILEE	Pink-yellow blend	HT	M	In cool weather it's an artful blend of pink and nearly white, but when the weather warms so do the colors—to light yellow and coppery pink. Stylish long buds slowly unfurl to full flowers that hold an attractive shape. Bronzy red new foliage.
SWARTHMORE	Cherry pink	HT	T	Fabulously long buds of cherry red with darker margins become very long-lasting open flowers of a lighter pink but still with the darker edge. Free flowering, upright bush.
THE DOCTOR	Rose pink	HT	L	Not a large or fast growing bush, and not always the easiest to grow well, but when it's happy can produce really huge, fragrant buds and satiny pink flowers. Prune lightly.
THE FAIRY	Pale pink	P	L	The individual flowers are unimportant, but the numbers of them per cluster create the effect. Bushes are low, spreading, very vigorous, with fern-like, disease-proof foliage.
TIFFANY	Warm pink	HT CL	T	AARS 1955. The large and long buds have the perfection of a finely cut jewel, and they open to lush, double, intensely fragrant blooms. At its best out of cool, damp regions. Upright.
VOGUE	Cherry-coral	F	M	AARS 1952. Slender, stylish buds suggested this rose be named after the *Vogue* models of similar style. Upright and bushy plants bear medium sized clusters of these very fragrant flowers.

ORANGE AND MULTICOLOR
(also see pages 47, 50, 52)

Montezuma   Mrs. Sam McGredy

Tropicana   Spartan

ROSE VARIETIES   49

ORANGE AND MULTICOLOR ROSES

(See color on pages 47, 49)

Name	Color	Type	Height	Description
CHICAGO PEACE	Pink-copper blend	HT	M	A color sport of 'Peace' in which all the virtues of foliage, plant, and magnificent flower form have been retained but in a more lively flower—bronzy yellow, deep pink, and copper.
CIRCUS PARADE	Orange buff-pink	F	M	A color sport of the floribunda 'Circus' in which the colors have intensified to a buff yellow with more pink and red in the open flower. Plants are bushy and compact but larger, with larger leaves.
COMMAND PERFORMANCE	Orange-scarlet	HT	T	AARS 1971. An offspring of 'Tropicana' that boasts a similar glowing orange color. As the long buds unfold, their petal edges roll back to give open blooms a star effect. Very vigorous, mildew prone.
CONTEMPO	Copper-orange	F	M	Noteworthy among floribundas for its orange-copper-gold color. Well formed, pointed buds and full, 2–3-inch blooms come singly or in clusters on a bushy plant.
FIRELIGHT	Orange-scarlet	HT	T	Ember-like dark orange-red buds are large and long pointed, opening to nonfading, luminous coral red blooms on long stems. Bushes are quite tall with light green foliage.
FLAMING PEACE	Red-gold bicolor	HT	M	Another color sport of 'Peace,' with similar plant and foliage but a dramatic color departure. As blooms open, petals are blood red inside with gold reverses; mature flowers are purple-red and buff.
FORTY-NINER	Red-yellow bicolor	HT	M	AARS 1949. A distinct bicolor, the outside of the petals is creamy yellow while the inside is a bright Chinese red that blues somewhat as it ages. Shapely buds on a compact, upright bush.
FRED EDMUNDS	Copper-orange	HT	L	Slim, bright burnt orange buds develop into informal blooms that gradually fade to apricot. Unusually attractive glossy dark green leaves clothe a short, bushy plant that is less winter hardy than many.
GINGER	Orange-scarlet	F	L	A less flashy 'Tropicana' orange-scarlet color brought down to a knee high bush. Rosette-shaped flowers come singly and in clusters. Fine dark green foliage and nearly thornless canes.
GOLDEN SLIPPERS	Orange and gold	F	L	AARS 1962. As the pointed gold buds open they reveal the petals' orange inner surfaces. In cool weather or partial shade the colors are brilliant and lasting. Spreading, few-thorned plants.
GRANADA	Red and yellow blend	GR	M	AARS 1964. Nasturtium red, light yellow, and pink blend together into notably fragrant and very long lasting flowers. Well-formed, slender buds often come in clusters. Holly-like, dark foliage.
HAWAII	Orange-coral	HT	T	Stylish orange buds turn into tropical coral-orange blooms that are color fast and fragrant. Grayed green leaves complement the flower color. Vigorous and tall.
INVITATION	Salmon-orange	HT	T	Long, tapered buds on a long, tapered plant of great vigor and productiveness. Salmon orange fading to salmon pink are the colors. Foliage is a good, glossy green and flowers are fragrant.
IRISH MIST	Orange-salmon	F	M	Perfect hybrid tea-style blooms of almost hybrid tea size are soft salmon orange. Bushy plant with dark green foliage profusely produces these blooms singly or in small clusters.
JOSEPH'S COAT	Red, orange, yellow	CL		The accent is on versatility: use it as a climber or as a free-standing shrub. Color changes from yellow buds through orange and red shadings to crimson mature blooms in floribunda-like clusters.

Eclipse *King's Ransom*

Irish Gold *Redgold*

Name	Color	Type	Height	Description
MARGO KOSTER	Light orange	P CL	L	Almost round buds are composed of many shell-like petals that open into small cupped flowers resembling ranunculus. Color is a soft coral orange. Large clusters of bloom on a twiggy, compact bush.
MEDALLION	Buff apricot	HT	T	AARS 1973. Everything about this rose is large, from the extra long buds to the open flowers, even to the plant. Buff-apricot in bud, the open flowers have pink tones. Upright.
MME. HENRI GUILLOT	Coral-red	HT CL	M	Open flowers often have been likened to coral colored camellias, so regular is their form. Buds are coral red and open quickly except in cool regions. Beautiful glossy leaves on a wide spreading bush.
MOJAVE	Burnt orange	HT	T	AARS 1950. Stylish burnt orange buds are veined a darker shade, open to 25-petalled light apricot orange blooms. Vigorous, very slender bushes have dark canes and glossy dark green leaves.
MONTEZUMA	Coral Orange	HT	T	Beautifully formed nearly red buds lighten as they open to coral salmon (or orange coral in warm weather). Robust plants are slightly spreading with leaves that start out bronzy red.
MRS. SAM McGREDY	Copper red and salmon	HT CL	L	Most widely planted in its climbing form which is more vigorous than the bush and with stronger stems. Flawless, classically tapered buds are copper-scarlet with salmon to apricot color on the petals' insides. New foliage is bronzy maroon passing to dark green.
OLDTIMER	Bronze apricot	HT	T	Very large blooms develop from long, streamlined buds— all petals having an elegant satin texture. Color is golden apricot with tints of bronze or copper. Leathery, pointed leaves, upright bush.
PICCADILLY	Scarlet-yellow bicolor	HT	M	A bright and cheerful bicolor, it is basically a light yellow with the inside of petals completely washed scarlet except at the bases. Colors fade to pink and cream. Beautiful bronze-tinted foliage.
PRESIDENT HERBERT HOOVER	Buff, orange, red blend	HT	T	Giant, vase-shaped bushes produce some of the longest cutting stems imaginable. Buff-gold is blended with pink and red in the outer petals. Beautifully formed blooms on sparsely foliaged bushes.
ROMAN HOLIDAY	Orange-red	F	L	AARS 1967. A tinge of yellow on the outside of petals adds extra sparkle to the bright red-orange, double flowers. Dark green foliage is good foil for the many flower clusters. Bushy.
ROYAL SUNSET	Orange blend	CL		Basically orange buds are of the best hybrid tea form and size, open to large, fairly double buff-apricot blooms that pale to a creamy peach in hot weather. Glossy deep green leaves.
SPARTAN	Salmon orange	F	M	Blooms are a little larger than the average floribunda. Burnt orange, well formed buds open to very full coral-orange flowers that have an "old-fashioned" look. Vigorous and upright bushes.
TALISMAN	Yellow-orange-copper blend	HT	M	A favorite bicolor for nearly half a century. Flat-topped buds are golden on the outside, copper-orange inside, and open to cream and pink blooms. Bright green foliage, upright.
TANYA	Orange	HT	M	Ruddy orange suffused apricot in bud, mostly apricot in the open flower. Petal edges curl under so that blooms have quilled appearance. Bushy, somewhat spreading plants.
TROPICANA	Orange-scarlet	HT CL	T	Forerunner of the fluorescent, unshaded orange colors. Medium sized pointed buds produce full, rather cupped open flowers either singly or in clusters. Vigorous, semi-spreading, and mildew-prone.
VALENCIA	Apricot-orange	HT	M	Slender orange buds produce fragrant apricot-orange open blooms of good size that pale quickly during hot weather. Sometimes variable performance but beautiful at its best.

YELLOW ROSES
(See color on pages 51, 54)

Name	Color	Type	Height	Description
AKEBONO	Yellow and pink blend	HT	T	Basically light yellow, but this color sometimes is so heavily infused with pink as to make it a blend. Large, well formed and slow opening blooms atop rather thin stems come on upright plants.
AMERICAN HERITAGE	Yellow, tinted pink	HT	T	AARS 1966. Long, slender creamy yellow buds are edged light red, and this color remains as the 50-petalled flower opens. Free blooming with bronzy new foliage. A slender plant, its height and great vigor come from parent 'Queen Elizabeth.'
APOLLO	Light Yellow	HT	T	AARS 1972. Lovely long, tapered buds open quickly to large blooms of about 35 petals with pleasing fragrance. Production is lavish on long stems. Dark green foliage clothes a very strong, upright bush.
ARLENE FRANCIS	Golden yellow	HT	M	A notably fragrant, clear golden yellow. Beautifully formed, long pointed buds develop into moderately double, large blooms. Bushes are somewhat spreading, mantled in glossy, dark green leaves.
BUCCANEER	Bright yellow	GR	T	Give this one plenty of room—it's extremely tall and willowy. Shining yellow, well shaped buds on long stems hold their bright color in the open flower. Dark green foliage.
CIRCUS	Yellow-red blend	F	L	AARS 1956. Yellow buds in the best hybrid tea style are blended with red at the edges; as blooms open, more red infuses the petals to give buff and pink shadings. Glossy dark foliage, spreading plant.
DIAMOND JUBILEE	Buff-yellow	HT	M	AARS 1948. Light buff yellow blooms open slowly and are at their best when half or more open; in poor weather the buds are not always attractive. Very fragrant, strong and upright.
ECLIPSE	Medium yellow	HT	M	An old favorite, loved for its long, stylish buds. Open flowers are not especially lovely, but bud production is plentiful on a very vigorous, upright bush with grayed green leaves.
GOLDEN GATE	Deep yellow	HT	M	Long, tapered golden buds unfurl in spiral fashion to deep yellow, long lasting blooms of about 30 petals. The plant is slightly spreading, with plenty of glossy foliage.
GOLDEN GIANT	Medium yellow	HT	T	A bulky giant of a bush with strong arching canes sporting distinctly large light green foliage. Bright, well formed buds fade little after opening, come singly or in small clusters. Abuse-resistant plant.
GOLDEN PRINCE	Golden yellow	HT	M	Beautiful deep golden yellow buds are sometimes tinged with red, open quickly to a lighter yellow. Upright bush is well clothed in large, shiny green foliage.
GOLDEN SCEPTER	Bright yellow	HT	T	Medium sized, slender buds of bright, luminous pure yellow open quickly but fade very little. Excellent for cutting as it's always in bloom. Very vigorous, slender growth with glossy, dark foliage.
GOLDEN SHOWERS	Daffodil yellow	CL		AARS 1957. Introduced as a pillar rose, but can be a full-fledged climber in mild climates. Pointed butter yellow buds and lighter, semi-double open blooms. Very free flowering with excellent foliage.
HIGH NOON	Golden yellow	CL		AARS 1948. Similar in many respects to 'Golden Showers'—a pillar or rampant climber, depending upon climate. Buds are flushed with red, and the entire effect is more golden than pure yellow.

Summer Sunshine (top left)
Sutter's Gold (top right)
Peace (right)

Yellow Roses (continued)

Name	Color	Type	Height	Description
IRISH GOLD	Light yellow	HT	M	Flawless full but pointed buds of pale yellow gradually unfurl to very double blooms tinged with pink in cool weather; petals become pointed at tips as edges recurve. Glossy bright green foliage.
KING'S RANSOM	Deep yellow	HT	M	AARS 1962. Classically formed long buds open symmetrically into unfading chrome yellow, 6-inch flowers. Vigorous, easy to grow plants adorned with dark, glossy leaves.
LEMON SPICE	Light yellow	HT	T	Light lemon yellow is the color, the spice is its intense fragrance. Fast opening, long pointed buds with stems sometimes not strong enough to hold them upright. Large, spreading bush.
LOWELL THOMAS	Deep yellow	HT	M	AARS 1944. For many years the standard bearer among bright, medium yellow roses with the ability to perform well in all regions. Long pointed buds, 5-inch double blooms, and an erect, compact bush.
McGREDY'S SUNSET	Yellow-orange blend	HT	L	A plant for the foreground: vigorous but low and spreading. Buds are deep yellow shaded red; open flower is globular at first, then becomes flat, with more blending of red and yellow to sunset hues.
McGREDY'S YELLOW	Light yellow	HT	M	Perfection in soft light yellow, especially in cool climates. Elegant long buds and well formed open flowers. Bushes are upright with bronze tinted leaves and distinctive large red thorns.
PAGLIACCI	Yellow, tinted red	GR	T	Yellow only in the bud, then full of surprises. Slender buds are edged in cerise, and as they unfold the pink color overtakes the petals until the yellow is gone. Upright, with large leaves.
PEACE	Yellow and pink blend	HT CL	M	AARS 1946. Full, ovoid buds are yellow touched with pink or red, gradually unfold to yellow petals widely edged pink. A glorious half to fully open bloom, very full and regular. Strong, spreading bush.
REDGOLD	Gold and red blend	F	L	AARS 1971. Golden yellow buds edged in red become less yellow as flowers open and the red suffuses more of the bloom. Nicely shaped buds on a compact, bushy, well foliaged plant.
ROYAL GOLD	Golden yellow	CL		Glowing yellow, perfect hybrid tea buds on a natural climber or pillar type—larger in mild regions. Blooms come singly or in small clusters and retain color and form as they open.
SAN DIEGO	Pale yellow	HT	M	The large, creamy yellow blooms are full and well-formed, most attractive when half or more open. Petal edges sometimes are tinted pink. Plants are bushy and somewhat spreading.
SUMMER SUNSHINE	Pure bright yellow	HT	M	The most brilliant pure yellow imaginable, both in bud and open bloom. Beautifully chiseled buds are complemented by shiny green, bronze tinted foliage. Plants are upright and bushy.
SUNBONNET	Bright yellow	F	L	Another good foreground plant with low, bushy growth. Bright, shapely buds and double flowers, singly or in clusters, with the fragrance of licorice. Glossy, dark green foliage.
SUTTER'S GOLD	Yellow-orange blend	HT	T	A powerfully fragrant blended yellow with elegant long buds. Most attractive in cool climates where its flowers open more slowly and hold color better. Long, dark stems and a strong, willowy bush.
WESTERN SUN	Deep yellow	HT	L	Well formed, full flowers of deep golden yellow open reliably in all weather, so are valuable in cool, damp regions. Upright and bushy with distinctive light green leaves.

Sterling Silver

Iceberg

WHITE AND LAVENDER
(also see pages 56, 58-60)

Angel Face

WHITE ROSES
(See color on pages 57, 59)

Name	Color	Type	Height	Description
BLANCHE MALLERIN	Pure white	HT	M	Buds are long pointed in the best hybrid tea form, opening to large full flowers with some fragrance. Best whenever weather is warm. Upright, vigorous bush.
GARDEN PARTY	Ivory	HT	M	AARS 1960. Finely crafted long ivory buds are tinted pink on the petal margins and this intensifies as they open to beautiful, full, stiffly perfect blooms. Vigorous, upright bush sometimes mildews.
ICEBERG	Pure white	FL	T	More of a large shrub than a typical floribunda. Well formed buds are long and pointed, while open flowers are nearly hybrid tea size. Vigorous, adaptable plant covered with healthy light green leaves.
IVORY FASHION	Ivory	FL	M	An aristocratic floribunda of hybrid tea refinement. Attractively pointed long buds open to semi-double, 4-inch blooms decorated with masses of golden stamens in the centers. Long lasting when cut.
JOHN F. KENNEDY	Greenish white	HT	T	Impeccably formed, long buds are distinctly tinged green in cool weather, otherwise are pure white with petals spiraling open to a beautifully formed, full bloom. Upright, and better in warm regions.
KAISERIN AUGUSTE VIKTORIA	Pure white	HT CL	M	A nineteenth-century product that still can keep company with the modern roses. Long, pointed, cream-white buds open to very full flowers wherever weather is not cool and damp. Vigorous and bushy.
MATTERHORN	Ivory	HT	T	AARS 1966. A mountain of a plant strictly for the background or for hedges. Well formed, yellow tinted buds give way to ivory-white open flowers sometimes with deeper color in the centers. Very vigorous.
MOUNT SHASTA	Pure white	GR	T	Another skyscraping plant, this has longer buds, larger flowers, and whiter color than 'Matterhorn.' Of grandiflora height and vigor, but a hybrid tea in all other respects. Good in cool areas.
PASCALI	Pure white	HT	T	Perfectly formed, medium sized buds and flowers can be depended on more than many other whites in all climates. Abundantly produced, they come on upright bushes with dark foliage.
SARATOGA	Pure white	F	L	AARS 1964. The emphasis is on performance. Vigorous, much branched, compact but somewhat spreading bushes continually produce clusters of fragrant, gardenia-like blossoms. Healthy, glossy green foliage.
SINCERA	Pure white	HT	M	Satin textured petals start out in a shapely, medium sized bud, then expand into a very well formed, full petaled open bloom that is fairly weather resistant for a white. Upright, vigorous plant.
SNOWBIRD	Creamy white	HT CL	L	Perfect form, medium size, slender stems, and a spreading plant strongly suggest the old tea roses. Available more often in its climbing form. Sure to open well in damp, foggy regions.
SUMMER SNOW	Pure white	HT CL	L	Not grown for perfection of individual blooms but for the mass beauty of sparkling white. Double, informal flowers come in large clusters on shiny leaved plants good for borders or low hedges.
TOUCH OF VENUS	Ivory	HT	T	Not quite white, as the blooms are blushed pink in the centers. Elegantly tapered buds open full, excellently formed, and fragrant. Bushes are upright and willowy.

Matterhorn (top)
John F. Kennedy (center left)
Ivory Fashion (lower left)
Pascali (below)

Name	Color	Type	Height	Description
VIRGO	Pure white	HT	L	Perfectly formed flowers and nationwide good performance established its reputation years ago as the most dependable white hybrid tea. Medium sized flowers and plant, and a profuse bloomer.
WHITE DAWN	Pure white	CL		Medium sized, fragrant blooms have the form of a gardenia. Lavish spring display, moderate bloom through summer, then another big burst in fall. Very vigorous and cold tolerant to around zero.
WHITE KNIGHT	Greenish white	HT	M	AARS 1958. Sculptured greenish-white buds develop into beautiful satiny white open flowers tolerant of damp weather. Bushes are vigorous and upright with light green, mildew-prone foliage.

LAVENDER ROSES

(See color on pages 56, 57)

Name	Color	Type	Height	Description
ANGEL FACE	Rosy lavender	F	L	AARS 1969. The deep lavender color is enlivened by rose tints and is beautifully complemented by bronze-tinged deep green foliage. Ruffled, very double blooms are very fragrant. Spreading bush.
BLUE HEAVEN	Lilac lavender	HT	M	Ovoid, lilac-lavender buds open to fully double blooms of silvery lavender to rose-purple with good fragrance. The vigorous, somewhat spreading plants have large, dark foliage.
BLUE MOON	Silvery lavender	HT	M	A virtually unchanging silvery lavender, from the long tapered buds to the fully open flowers. Long stemmed, fragrant flowers come on upright bushes with dark foliage.
HEIRLOOM	Lavender-magenta	HT	M	The darkest color of these lavender varieties, this has lilac to purple buds opening to magenta flowers that lighten to lilac as they age. Fragrant, with medium sized, pointed buds.
INTERMEZZO	Lavender	HT	L	Clear lavender color in a large, well formed, very full flower. Medium sized blossoms are carried on a vigorous, compact, rather short plant with a surplus of thorns.
KÖLNER KARNEVAL	Silvery lavender	HT	M	Loosely formed open flowers develop from shapely silver-lavender buds of a slightly darker tone than 'Blue Moon.' Vigorous and bushy plants have shiny, dark green leaves.
LADY X	Pink-lavender	HT	T	The tallest and huskiest plant of these lavender roses, but the color is the least blue of any of them. Long, elegant, pale lavender-pink buds unfurl gracefully to full, double flowers.
LILAC CHARM	Lilac	F	L	Single flowers to 3 inches across are decorated with a mass of golden stamens in the center of each. Free blooming, in small clusters. Spreading, branching bushes have very dark foliage.
SILVER STAR	Silvery lavender	HT	T	Attractively long-pointed buds open slowly to 5-inch, double blossoms, with only slight fragrance. The upright bushes are vigorous and clothed in medium green foliage.
SONG OF PARIS	Lavender	HT	M	Full, fragrant flowers from ovoid buds are nearly the same lavender as 'Sterling Silver' but without the silvery quality. Flowers open best in warm weather. Bush is vigorous and spreading.
STERLING SILVER	Silvery lavender	HT CL	M	A delicious, "old rose" fragrance emanates from the delicate silvery lavender, ruffled and cup-shaped blossoms. Tends to produce floribunda-like clusters. Bush is moderately vigorous; prune lightly.

SHRUB AND OLD GARDEN ROSES

Name	Color	Type*	Height	Description
ALFRED DE DALMAS	Blush pink	M	M	1855. Sometimes catalogued as 'Mousseline.' The double, blush pink flowers fade to nearly white in sun. These are in clusters of well-mossed buds in floribunda-like profusion on bushy plants that are quite compact for a moss rose. May flower again after its spring burst.
AMERICAN BEAUTY	Cerise red	HP	M	1875. An almost legendary nostalgic favorite and the rose responsible for the popularity of long-stemmed red florist roses. Globular buds open to powerfully fragrant, smoky carmine full-petaled blooms.
AUSTRIAN COPPER	Gold and flame	S	T	Before 1590. This date is merely its year of introduction to cultivation; it is the species *Rosa foetida bicolor*. Single, 1–2-inch flowers are copper-orange on the face of petals, gold on the reverse. Flowers in spring only, but lavishly. Somewhat arching, 5–6 foot bushes; distinctive, ferny foliage.
BLANC DOUBLE DE COUBERT	White	R	T	1892. Rugosa foliage is thick, characteristically ridged, and impervious to disease. This variety has loose, pure white and fairly double flowers of a poppy-like texture. Bright orange hips develop after flowers fade. Spreading plants may reach 6 feet tall, and they bloom throughout the season.
CORNELIA	Coral pink	S	T	1925. Coral pink to apricot, small, fluffy blooms recur continually during the year in large clusters. Foliage is a complementary bronzy green. Growth is to 8 feet.
DEUIL DE PAUL FONTAINE	Maroon red	M	M	1873. Round, mossy buds open to 2-inch flowers packed with petals of an unusual purplish red with brown shadings. Foliage is dark green but the "moss" is a contrasting red. Plants reach about 4 feet and bloom throughout the season.
DUCHESSE DE BRABANT	Delicate pink	T	M	1857. More cold-tolerant than the majority of tea roses. The double, cupped blooms vary from pearly pink to deep rose and come continually on a vigorous, spreading bush that, in time, may reach 5 feet high and wide.
F. J. GROOTEN-DORST	Red	R	M	1918. Plants are very robust and quite cold-tolerant, with the characteristic dark, ribbed and wrinkled rugosa foliage. The flowers, however, are unique: small, very double, with all petal edges fringed so they look like carnations. The color is cherry red and they come in clusters.
FRAU KARL DRUSCHKI	Pure white	HP	T	1901. Long, pointed buds sometimes are tinged pink but always open to sparkling white, double blossoms. A rose classic that still is contemporary. In mild regions it can be used as a climber, its canes will grow so long. Flowers open reasonably well even in damp climates.
FRÜHLINGS-MORGEN	Pink and yellow	S	T	1942. Very vigorous, arching, 6-foot bushes produce most of their flowers in spring. These are single, yellow edged with cherry pink and have contrasting maroon stamens in the centers. Foliage is a dark bluish green. In autumn, the hips turn brilliant red.
GENERAL JACQUEMINOT	Dark red	HP	T	1853. Somewhere in the ancestry of virtually all red hybrid teas today, the "Jack Rose" still compares favorably with its 20th century kin. Velvety red, somewhat cupped blooms develop from well formed, darker red buds on long stems. Very fragrant, and vigorous to about 5 feet.
HARISON'S YELLOW	Yellow	S	T	1830. A vigorous 6-foot shrub with dark, thorny canes and fern-like foliage. One blooming season in spring brings forth clouds of small sulfur yellow, double flowers. Brought West by the pioneers, it can be found growing "wild" in many old towns and farmsites.

*B=Bourbon, D=Damask, HP=hybrid perpetual, M=moss, R=rugosa, S=shrub, T=tea.

Will Alderman

Mme. Hardy

Mrs. John Laing

Thérèse Bugnet

Deuil de Paul Fontaine

Name	Color	Type	Height	Description
LA FRANCE	Pink	HT	M	1867. Presumably the first hybrid tea, and modern rose history begins with its introduction. Long pointed buds are silvery pink inside, bright pink outside. Open flowers are double, cupped and fragrant. Vigorous bushes, 4–5 feet.
LA REINE VICTORIA	Rose pink	B	T	1872. Throughout the blooming season, the tall, slender plants produce very double, cupped to globular blooms in shades of rose pink, deeper on outer petals. Very fragrant.
MME. HARDY	Pure white	D	M	1832. Its special beauty is in the open flowers which are cupped to flat, each packed with carefully arranged petals around a green center. Clusters of these fragrant, pure white flowers appear in spring only, on a 6-foot bush.
MRS. JOHN LAING	Pink	HP	M	1887. Plump but shapely buds curl back their petal edges, then open in very modern style to full, fragrant flowers on good stems. Will make long, arching canes but is not as rampant as many other hybrid perpetuals.
NEVADA	Cream	S	T	1927. Long, arching canes of this 7-foot shrub carry pink-tinted white blooms all along their length in spring, then repeat flowering throughout the season. Individual flowers are nearly single, 4 inches across.
PAUL NEYRON	Deep pink	HP	M	1869. The term "cabbage rose" is perfectly embodied in this flower. Deep, slightly bluish-pink blooms are loaded with row upon row of petals opening from fat buds. Long stems and healthy lettuce green foliage. Canes are long and tall, arching somewhat.
PRAIRIE FIRE	Scarlet	S	T	1960. The scarlet-cerise, semi-double flowers scream for attention. These come in clusters, set off by shiny dark green foliage. Bushes are quite cold-tolerant, about 6 feet tall.
ROGER LAMBELIN	Maroon and white	HP	M	1890. A character among the hybrid perpetuals. Each large, double bloom is deep crimson with wavy petals edged in white. Vigorous bushes are short enough to associate with hybrid teas.
SAFRANO	Buff yellow	T	T	1839. For many years this was the only large flowered, double rose with golden yellow blossoms. Where winters are mild it will grow into a 6-foot, bushy shrub covered all year with attractive buff-apricot to yellow blooms from pointed buds.
SOUVENIR DE LA MALMAISON	Flesh pink	B	L	1843. Cupped, flesh pink blooms are so double that cool, damp climates may not be able to develop their full beauty. They epitomize the image of old roses with their form, petallage, and fragrance. Bushy, medium sized plants flower continuously.
SPARRIESHOOP	Pink	S	T	1953. Large, graceful, single blossoms are borne all season in clusters on a very vigorous and tall plant that can be used as a shrub or a climber. Healthy, glossy foliage is bronze-tinted at first.
THERESE BUGNET	Lilac pink	S	T	1950. Developed in Canada to withstand winters there with no protection. Clusters of slender buds open to very double lilac pink flowers that have a fluffy, informal quality. Blooms come all season on 4–6 foot, healthy shrubs.
WILL ALDERMAN	Lilac pink	R	M	1949. A typical rugosa hybrid with wrinkled, ridged, glossy foliage on a rounded, dense bush that reaches about 5 feet. Lilac pink, 3-inch blooms appear all season and are followed by large, tomato-red hips in fall.
ZEPHIRINE DROUHIN	Bright pink	B	T	1868. A completely thornless climber that also will double as a relaxed shrub. Bright carmine pink buds are attractively pointed and open to good sized, semi-double blooms carried in small clusters. Plants bloom all year and have light green, copper tinted foliage.

THREE CLASSIC landscape examples suggest the versatility of roses and the colorful effects they can provide. One standard plant (above) enlivens an otherwise bare wall; decorating a weathered wood fence (below left) is a climbing hybrid tea in harmonizing colors; timeless combination (below right) is rose garden and lawn.

Roses In the Landscape

VIRTUALLY no other popular garden ornamental can come close to matching the versatility of the rose. Its use in your garden really is limited by only three factors: suitability of your garden for roses in general, your garden's size, and your imagination.

Reduced to basic, clinical description, a rose is a flowering shrub. But a remarkable shrub it is, encompassing a great variety of growth types and foliage and flower forms; a wide range of colors; a long flowering season; decorative fruits; and nearly limitless combinations of these variables. Do you need a bedding plant that will flower almost continually yet never need replanting? Then choose one of the miniatures or a lower growing floribunda. Even some of the low hybrid teas can serve this purpose. You can plan hedges of any size and description: low and profuse with floribundas or polyanthas or miniatures, high and showy with grandifloras, or informal and nearly impenetrable with some of the shrub varieties and species. Miniature roses—perfect replicas of modern hybrid teas and floribundas—can border a planting of larger roses or other flowers, as well as grow in containers either indoors or outside. Fences, walls, arbors, and trellises traditionally are strongholds of rose display, but a number of those that you train up and over also will grow down and out—as ground or slope covers. The showy orange fruits or "hips" on some climbers and shrub types provide a splash of autumn color that rivals the beauty of the spring bloom.

Shrub roses, left to go their own exuberant ways with a minimum of trimming, can provide a backdrop to other rose plantings, at the same time tying the entire plan together because of the similar foliage and flowers. Some of the repeat-flowering shrub roses easily could replace other flowering shrubs, such as lilacs, that bloom but once each year.

Rose growing need not be limited to the open garden. For close-up enjoyment, bring them onto your patio or terrace. Floribundas and miniatures are tailor-made for small patio planting areas or raised beds; the shelter from wind or winter cold provided there also may be what is needed to bring out the best in one of the repeat-flowering climbers. And don't overlook the value of roses in large containers. Any of the newer miniatures or floribundas with hybrid tea-like flowers (or some of the shorter hybrid teas themselves) can become beautiful conversation pieces when displayed this way. In containers you can easily give them the regular watering, fertilizing and spraying or dusting that will encourage them to perform to perfection. See pages 27-28 for details of growing roses in containers.

Not only the choice of rose but also how you use it can influence the mood of your garden picture. Evenly spaced plants in geometrically shaped rose beds present a more formal, organized look—the precision of a military formation with the beauty of a chorus line. The same roses used in flowing curves and irregularly shaped planting areas appear more casual, relaxed, informal, or "natural." A row of standards, whether straight or curving, will give direction to the eye and to anyone strolling through the garden, but just one can provide *emphasis*. Oftentimes, a single, well-groomed standard—strategically placed—or just one pillar rose can be as eye-catching as a bedful of mixed varieties.

The examples go on and on. But before you decide to plant any kind of rose, first consider what they need in order to flourish. Then you can plan to place them wherever in your garden they are most likely to succeed.

WHERE TO GROW ROSES

A rose's requirements are not difficult to understand or to satisfy. To ignore them, however, is to risk disappointment and do an injustice to a beautiful flower. By keeping the following points in mind when planning locations for your roses, you should be rewarded by years of increasing pleasure as your roses prosper.

• Roses, once planted, do not like to be disturbed often and are a greater chore to move as years pass and plants become larger. Plan ahead.

• Roses like sun and require it to flourish. See that they receive it for at least six hours each day, preferably in the morning. In cool or frequently-overcast climates they'll do best if planted where they can receive sunshine all day. In regions having intense summer heat, plant roses where they'll be shaded from the scorching glare and heat of afternoon sun; filtered shade cast by high trees growing at some distance from the roses is good. (Roses will *grow* in shade. But plants there usually are disappointingly leggy with sparse bloom—while mildew and rust are more troublesome and more difficult to control.)

• Avoid planting roses in windswept places. Strong or continuous winds spoil flowers and cause excessive transpiration from leaves so that you have to water more often than normally would be needed.

• Roses like the soil to themselves. Be wary of planting near trees and shrubs for their roots have an insidious habit of reaching into rose beds for the better supply of water and nutrients there, stealing a good portion from the roses.

• Rose soil must drain well, though it should be moisture retentive.

When planning where to plant your roses, keep in mind the added enjoyment you can have if they are visible from inside the house. Whether a bed of roses or a single specimen, their value to you increases the more often you can see them.

Another point you might tuck away in the back of your mind is an expansion plan. Your first success with roses often will whet your appetite to grow more, and each year brings alluring new varieties to add to your garden. If you can, allow ground room for expansion of your first plantings or think of other areas you could develop for roses.

Layout and Spacing

After you select a place for roses, your next concern will be the garden layout. How far apart should you plant the bushes? With so many attractive varieties available, you may be tempted to buy all that sound interesting and then crowd them into a big, sunny bed. The best advice, if you are in danger of succumbing, is this: don't. If you realize that all roses probably will need some spraying, fertilizing, and pruning, you'll understand the value of planning for easy maintenance. The wide, deep, and crowded rose bed will become, in a few years, a colorful thicket which will only discourage you from giving plants the attention they deserve. Easiest to care for are plantings that you can reach from at least two sides—just wide enough that plants in the center can be reached from either side. This makes it easy for you to perform all routine maintenance without walking through the roses and compacting the soil around them. If you plant in a bed that abuts a fence or wall, your work will be simpler if the planting is two, or at the most three, bushes deep. You'll also find that if you plant in parallel rows, staggered spacing makes for easier maintenance than when one bush is directly behind another.

If your intended rose bed will be bordered by lawn, you can do two things to make the unavoidable edging task easier. First, plan for as few beds as possible; this cuts down on the number of feet of edges you'll have to trim. Second, a brick, concrete, concrete block, or wood mowing strip between lawn and bed will keep the bed edge even and simplify mowing right up to the edge.

How far apart you plant your roses depends upon your climate and the particular roses you plant. Where winter cold forces you to prune down to 1-2 feet each spring and the following growing season is short, bushes seldom achieve the bulk that they do in warmer regions. Planted 24 to 30 inches apart, hybrid teas and grandifloras will fill in the bed well without becoming tangled. Throughout most of the South, Southwest, and West, hybrid teas and grandifloras normally will go about 36 inches apart. Where there is little or no frost to force definite winter dormancy (such as in parts of southern California, the Gulf Coast, and Florida), rose bushes grow so prodigiously all year that they need to be planted up to 48 inches or more apart. Most floribundas generally are smaller but bushy plants and are massed in plantings for group effect: except for especially vigorous, spreading varieties space them about 24 inches apart in colder climates, 30 inches apart where winters are relatively mild.

Most shrub and many "old garden roses" need more elbow room than modern hybrids, but just how much more depends upon the growth habit of the varieties or species you intend to plant. From five to six feet apart is a reasonable general guide, perhaps a little farther for any varieties whose canes you plan to peg down in order to get bloom all along their length (see page 73).

MAKE THE MOST of garden space by using roses that provide bloom at different levels. Patio planting (left) employs climbers on adjacent house wall; standards carry bloom over floribunda and low hybrid tea bushes.

As you spend pleasant hours selecting roses for your intended garden, look past the glowing color descriptions and check for information on growth habits. It's crucial to choose the right roses for your plan. A rampant, 30-foot climber like 'Silver Moon' or 'Belle Portugaise' will be entirely unsuited to a 10-foot-wide patio wall, for example, whereas a climber of moderate growth or a pillar rose would do the landscape job admirably. Similarly, don't put a modest little bush like 'Picture' behind a robust giant like 'Queen Elizabeth': you'll never see it.

COLOR HARMONY

Some gardeners feel that all nature's colors combine pleasantly. If you are one of them, pass over to the next section. But if the idea of a screaming orange 'Tropicana' next to the deep, cold pink of 'Miss All-American Beauty' makes you grit your teeth, then you'll want to give some thought to establishing a good-neighbor color policy in your rose bed.

Colors that need the greatest care in placement are the pure, unshaded, full tones: clear orange and orange-scarlet, bright red, deep yellow, and dark pink. The even orange of 'Tropicana' is more difficult to harmonize than the blended orange-copper of 'Mojave', for example, because 'Tropicana', being entirely one shade, almost always contrasts with its neighbors, whereas a yellow blend may pick up some of the paler orange tones of 'Mojave' and tie the two together. Some dazzling contrasts can be established by placing some of the pure, bright colors side by side (such as yellow next to

red or orange), but too much of this assaults the eye rather than pleases it. You also can use white roses to contrast with these bright, clear colors, but if overdone this practice creates a spotty effect.

The easiest colors to mix throughout your rose planting are cream, buff, light yellow, yellow blends, pink blends, and yellow and pink combinations. These can buffer the strong colors and intercede between unrelated colors to tie them together. The soft yellow and pink of 'Peace', for example, can step in between magenta and orange varieties to prevent an otherwise strong clash. The lavender and mauve roses associate well with these soft and blended colors, as well as with the dark, rich reds and most deep yellows. Bicolors can be part of a stunning grouping if planted with varieties that match the colors on both sides of their petals.

Any number of attractive or even dramatic color effects can be achieved with just one or two roses against a house wall or garden fence, choosing the rose and background for harmony or contrast. For a bright, clean appearance what could beat red roses against a white wall or white picket fence? You can have brilliance but richness with the 'Tropicana'-orange color backed by stained redwood or cedar. The driftwood gray of weathered wood is a harmonious foil for apricot and salmon colored varieties. Pink roses against a gray surface, or pink or lavender roses next to a light green house are pleasing pastel combinations.

In the final analysis, color groupings are still a matter of individual taste. But don't be afraid to try some of the strong, clear colors because you feel they may be difficult to handle. They can add life and sparkle to a planting that might otherwise be pleasant but bland.

Seasonal Maintenance for Healthy Plants

PROBABLY no other aspect of rose growing has aroused as much controversy as the subject of pruning. For over half a century, battle lines have been drawn between the advocates of light pruning and those who champion hard cutting back. During these years, much trial-and-error data has been accumulated. The conclusions from this (plus a better understanding of plant physiology and rose ancestries) have favored the proponents of light-to-moderate pruning. To understand why this is the case, let's first learn basically how a plant's roots, stems, and leaves function together, and then take a look at the history of rose pruning.

HOW A PLANT GROWS

The roots, stems, and leaves of a rose plant all work together toward the plant's continued growth, productiveness, and increase in size. Roots, of course, not only anchor the plant in the soil, but also absorb dissolved nutrients from water present in the soil. These nutrients are then carried upward and throughout the stems of the plant in specialized cells. At the same time, leaves are taking in carbon dioxide from the atmosphere and converting it into sugars and other "foods" which can be transported throughout the plant in another type of specialized cell.

Not all absorbed nutrients and synthesized substances (such as sugars) are used immediately, however; some are stored in tissues of roots and stems to be used at some later time. Proteins, for example, are put together from glucose sugar which is produced by the leaves; they are vital to the production of new plant cells as the plant grows. These proteins can be stored in the wood and bark cells toward the end of the growing season when no appreciable new growth is being produced but while leaves still are manufacturing sugars. When growth resumes in spring, the plant draws upon this stored protein because there are no leaves to start immediately producing proteins needed for growth.

If you prune heavily, you impose several hardships on your rose plant. You have thrown away much of the plant's stored reserves (those in the stems) for starting off spring growth. This forces the plant to rely upon reserves stored in the roots for the initial growth push. And since the root system enlarges in proportion to the size of the plant—(remember, the leaves manufacture "foods" that contribute to the growth of the entire plant) —continual heavy pruning results in a small root system with only a small amount of stored nutrients to call upon in spring. Heavily pruned plants produce a limited amount of growth at the first flush; this means fewer leaves will be there to begin manufacturing growth substances for additional new growth.

DEVELOPMENT OF ROSE PRUNING

Rose pruning as the annual ritual we know today grew out of the 19th century development of varieties which had large, well-formed flowers lending themselves to individual exhibition at flower shows. Most of these exhibition varieties were found among the tea roses and the recently-emerged hybrid perpetual class (see pages 8-9). In order to produce the really large blooms which invariably were the award winners, rose growers would severely prune their bushes every year, believing that all of the plants' energies would be concentrated into producing just a few really magnificent flowers on long stems. Plant longevity was not as important to these exhibitors as was the winning of prizes; if a good ribbon-winner proved to be "weak" in the garden, he would replace it with new plants every few years.

What was overlooked in the slavish adherence to low pruning was a consideration of the *natural* growth habit of the roses being pruned. For simplicity, you can assume there are two growth types: those that produce new wood freely from the base and that will, on their own roots, spread into large clumps; and others that tend to build up a structure of old wood and produce more new growth from old wood than from the base. By mid-19th century, rose ancestries already were something of a mixed bag, but the hybrid perpetuals tended to fall into the first group, whereas tea roses definitely were in the second category. Hybrid teas, then, inherited from their tea ancestry the inclination to build up a woody plant structure. You will notice this particularly in some varieties (such as 'Charlotte Armstrong') that tend to form a framework of canes in their first few years in the garden and then build most new growth from these canes rather than from the bud union.

Around 1900 a major hybridizing breakthrough occurred which has influenced in a dramatic way the appearance and constitution of modern hybrid teas. This was the successful introduction of the species *Rosa foetida* (through its variety 'Persian Yellow') into the new hybrid tea class (see page 9). Not only did this species carry the yellow, orange, flame, and copper shades into hybrid teas, but also it brought its dislike for *any* pruning and its tendency to die back if cut into severely. Even today, many older varieties in these colors make much better garden plants if only lightly cut back.

Some hybrid teas that occur in both bush and climbing forms have had the reputation of being "better" as climbers. In some cases this is because of the climber's increased vigor, but very often it is simply because every year at pruning time the climber always is left with its entire cane length, whereas the bush is "pruned" severely. Allowed to build on old wood, the climber becomes larger and more prolific each year; the bush, on the other hand, has to make a relatively new start every spring.

HOW TO PRUNE HYBRID TEAS, GRANDIFLORAS, AND FLORIBUNDAS

The objectives of pruning are simply to promote a symmetrical bush, to encourage new growth, and to remove any diseased, damaged, or dead wood. Regardless of

PROTECT PRUNING CUTS—especially those to the bud union and all large-diameter ones—with special pruning paint.

where you live, here are a few basic pruning guidelines which should get you through any pruning job on the popular bush roses: hybrid teas, grandifloras, and floribundas. Additional tips for climbers, shrub, and species roses are on pages 72-73.

• Remove all dead wood and all weak, twiggy branches. If an older cane produced nothing but weak growth, remove it at the bud union.

• Open up the center of the bush by removing all branches that cross through the center. This gives you a "vase shaped" plant (a slender or a fat vase, depending on how upright or spreading the variety grows) without a profusion of twigs and leaves in the middle where insects and diseases could hide out and flourish. Note: rosarians in very hot climates often just shorten the branches that cross through the center. These will produce enough leaves to thoroughly shield canes from the scorching sun.

• Remove up to 1/3 of the length of all growth that was new during the year. To develop really large, specimen shrubs in the mild-winter areas of the South and West, don't cut into live new growth of the past season that is much bigger around than a lead pencil.

If you live where winter protection is necessary and you use a method that requires reducing the bush size to fit the protector, you almost surely will remove more than 1/3 of the past year's growth. In this case, try to not reduce the height any further in spring unless there has been winter kill below your original cuts. Whatever winter protection you may use, you'll have to cut out *all* damaged wood regardless of how low this leaves your bushes. Even though a cane may be green on the outside, if the center is brown, it is damaged. Prune all stems and canes back to wood that is light green to cream-white in the center.

• Make all cuts at a 45-degree angle close above a leaf bud that points toward the outside of the plant; the lowest point should be on the side of the stem opposite the bud, but not lower than the bud itself.

• Paint all cuts larger than lead-pencil size (and particularly all cuts to the bud union) with a sealing compound. Various asphalt preparations and orange shellac are sold by many nurseries.

Timing and Tools

When is the best time for rose pruning? You'll find that for most modern roses it is toward the end of the dormant season when growth buds along the canes begin to swell. Where winter temperatures are mild, this can be as early as January. In the "ice box" regions of the northeast, central, and mountain states you won't think about it until late March or April. In general, you should do the pruning in winter or early spring but not so early that the new growth which follows will be caught by late frosts. In areas where winter lingers and its chill trades off with spring temperatures during the transitional months of March or April, gardeners often rely upon two indicators for when to prune. Thirty days before the last expected killing frost generally is a safe time; ask your county agricultural agent for this average date. Or when forsythia comes into bloom, you can figure the time is ripe.

To do the job well, you need two tools: sharp pruning shears and a pruning saw. Although the shears will take care of most of the work, you'll need the saw (a small keyhole type or coping saw) for removing larger canes and those in areas that are awkward for shears. For the cleanest cuts, use the scissor-action shears with a curved steel cutting blade. Anvil type shears (in which the cutting is done by one blade against a flat metal surface) are easy to use but even when sharp will bruise the canes.

Pruning Aftercare

A thorough rose garden cleanup should be an annual routine, and directly after the final pruning is the easiest time for it. First, remove any leaves that remain on your rose plants. Then rake up and discard all old leaves, prunings, and any other debris that is on the ground or around the bases of the bushes: Insect eggs and some disease spores may be carried from one year to the next on old or dead leaves in the rose garden.

Right after you clean up the rose beds, spray the pruned bushes and the ground around them with lime-sulfur (calcium polysulfide) used at the dormant season strength listed on the spray's label as a final hedge against insect eggs and disease spores that may have remained on the plants or the soil's surface.

Other Ways to Regulate Growth

After new growth is under way in early spring, check over the new shoots that are emerging to see what directions they are taking. If any appear to be poorly located or unnecessary (crossing through the center of the bush, for example) break or rub them out. By eliminating this growth you conserve the plant's energy for the strong new shoots that are well placed; you also simplify your pruning operation the next year. Sometimes two or three new shoots will grow from one leaf axil. When you notice this, carefully rub out all but the strongest one.

During the flowering season, you will be removing flowers from your bushes—some for decoration in the house, the rest just to tidy up the plants. Actually, any removal of flowers is a bit of pruning, too, with a few guidelines of its own. If you remember that the leaves are helping to provide nutrients for the plants (see page 68), you'll realize the need for leaving a good supply on the bush. When you want a few long-stemmed beauties for inside, cut each stem so that you leave *at least* two sets of leaves on the branch from which you cut the flower. Or, when you remove faded blooms from the bushes, cut down only as far as necessary to keep the bush well-shaped—usually to the first five-leaflet leaf that points away from the bush's center.

New rose bushes and weak or small plants that you're trying to build up need all possible leaves to manufacture foods. With these plants, just snap off the faded flowers and cut no blossoms with stems for the house.

If you can bring yourself to do it, remove all (or all but one or two) flower buds on newly planted bushes for their first cycle of bloom. This will direct all their initial energies into root, leaf, and stem production.

HOW TO PRUNE CLIMBING ROSES

Several distinct growth and flowering habits fall under the category "climbing rose." What they all have in common is long, flexible canes that produce flowers from eyes along their length. For their first two or three years in your garden, your work with any of the climbers will be to train them (see page 73). Then, after their growth patterns are established and some wood has matured, you can think of how to prune them.

Climbing Hybrid Teas

Most climbing roses sold today can be classed as climbing hybrid teas. They bear the characteristic shapely buds throughout the entire flowering season from spring through fall. Many of these are simply climbing sports of familiar bush roses and carry the same name preceded by "Climbing." The same is true for some grandifloras and floribundas.

After you plant one of these climbers, leave it unpruned for the next two or three years: it takes that long for plants to become established and produce strong

BASIC PRUNING FUNDAMENTALS

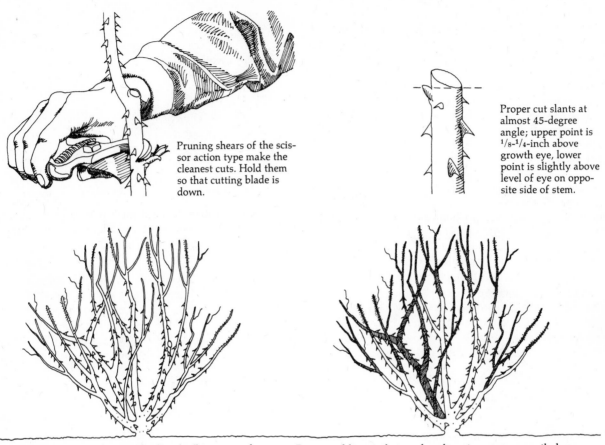

Pruning shears of the scissor action type make the cleanest cuts. Hold them so that cutting blade is down.

Proper cut slants at almost 45-degree angle; upper point is $1/8$-$1/4$-inch above growth eye, lower point is slightly above level of eye on opposite side of stem.

Ready for pruning, the dormant bush is leafless or nearly so. Note the amount of stems and their varying thicknesses.

Remove old canes that produced no strong new growth, branches crossing through bush's center, weak stems. Trim canes.

In mild climates, healthy growth should not be reduced by more than one-third. This is moderate to light pruning.

In areas where winter damage occurs, remove all dead and injured wood, leaving bush only $1/2$–$1/3$ the size it was in fall.

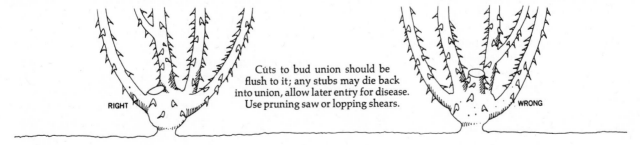

Cuts to bud union should be flush to it; any stubs may die back into union, allow later entry for disease. Use pruning saw or lopping shears.

RIGHT

WRONG

climbing canes. During this period, just remove all dead canes and branches, weak growth, and spent flowers; tie new canes into position as they mature (see page 73).

In several years' time, the plant will consist solely of long canes produced after you planted it in your garden. From these canes will come side branches (laterals) that will bear the flowers. Your pruning objectives are two-fold: to encourage growth of more flowering laterals and to stimulate production of new canes to gradually replace the oldest and less productive ones. (Varieties differ in this respect; some will always throw out new canes from the base each year, whereas others build up a more woody structure and produce most long new cane growth from higher on the plant.) Therefore, don't cut back the long canes at all unless any of them are growing too long for the allotted space. Whenever any long canes or branches grow in a direction contrary to what you want, first try to train them into place. Only if this won't work, remove them entirely (but remember—these long growths produce the flowering laterals).

For annual pruning, remove only the old and obviously unproductive wood. Then cut back to two or three eyes all of the laterals that bore flowers during the last year. The best blooms are produced on laterals growing from two or three-year-old wood.

During the flowering season, just remove all spent blooms, cutting back to a strong eye two or three leaves away from the flowering shoot's point of origin.

Large-Flowered Climbers

These roses have just those two features in common: fairly large flowers and the climbing growth habit. Some have hybrid tea-like blooms, others resemble floribundas, and a few even look like sophisticated wild roses. Some will bloom but once a year, whereas others repeat throughout summer and fall—and it is their blooming habits that are your best guide to pruning. For the first two or three years in your garden, all should receive the same treatment as recommended on page 73 for climbing hybrid teas.

Climbers like 'Dr. W. Van Fleet' and 'Paul's Scarlet Climber' that have only one flowering period should receive most of their pruning after their bloom. They flower on wood produced after their *last* year's flowering, so a dormant season pruning just throws away potential blooming wood. After they flower, cut out the least productive old canes and any weak, old, or entangling branches. New canes will grow from the base and low down on the remaining canes, and strong new laterals will grow from farther out on the older canes that you leave. From this new growth come most of the branches that will carry next year's flowers.

The large-flowered climbers that repeat their bloom throughout the year produce good flowering wood from new canes and laterals as well as from wood more than a year old. This group includes such favorites as 'Don Juan,' 'Golden Showers,' 'Joseph's Coat,' 'Kassel,' and 'New Dawn.' Prune these just as you would the climbing hybrid teas (see page 70).

With the once-blooming varieties among these natural climbers, little good is done by removing spent flowers or flower clusters. Some varieties may produce secondary blooms from the midst of old flower clusters or from just below them. Many go on to develop colorful and very decorative hips.

Pillar Roses

Two sorts of climbing roses are grown as flowering pillars up to about ten feet tall. One is the hybrid tea or floribunda climber which grows short climbing canes (about 8-10 feet long). The other is a natural pillar type which grows 6-10 foot upright canes that will flower along their length. Pruning objectives and methods are the same as for climbing hybrid teas; the principal difference is that you will train long new growth upright.

Ramblers

Each year after spring bloom, rambler roses produce many long, vigorous, and limber canes from the base of the plant. Next spring's flowers come from this new growth. Flowers are typically small, but in large clusters or trusses and come only once annually. This spring flower display, however, can be overwhelming.

Wait to prune ramblers until flowering has finished and new growth is underway. Then cut out canes that just flowered and show no sign of producing any long, vigorous new growth. As the new canes mature, train them into position.

PRUNING SHRUB AND OLD GARDEN ROSES

The durable and venerable rose species and old varieties represent such a diversity of types and growth habits that it is difficult to make many generalizations. Most, however, are vigorous growers that may need some thinning and shaping each year but very little actual cutting back. Since most of these roses are used for specimen shrubs or hedges, the primary pruning should be directed to trimming and shaping them to fit their places in the landscape picture. Cut back any shoots which depart unattractively from the general pattern of the plant; remove any old canes that produced little new growth or flowers, and any weak wood.

The shrub and old garden roses which have one flowering period per year bloom on the growth that they produced after the last year's bloom season. To prune these roses when you would your hybrid teas is to sacrifice some of their potential display. Wait until after they finish flowering; then you can cut out the least productive old wood. You also may shorten long new canes; this will encourage them to put forth more lateral growth on which the next spring's blossoms will come.

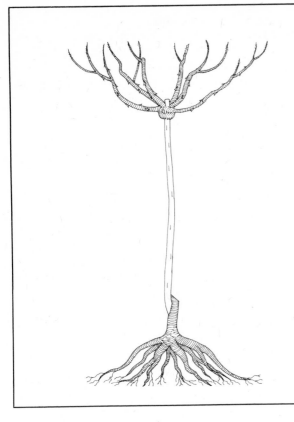

STANDARDS AND HOW TO PRUNE THEM

The quintessence of the rose propagator's art is the standard—popularly called a "tree rose." As the diagram shows, it consists of three separate parts: the understock, a stem or trunk, and the head. Onto any good understock the propagator buds a rose that will quickly produce a long, thick cane. A year after this cane grows and is trained upright, it is budded with a popular hybrid tea or floribunda.

A standard's trunk is its most vulnerable part. Always give each plant a sturdy stake at planting time, placed close to the trunk and extending several inches into the head. Metal rods or pipes are the most durable; if you prefer wood, use a decay-resistant sort such as redwood. Standard trunks are susceptible to sun-scalding unless they are shaded. One way to avoid this is to place the stake on the sunny side of the trunk—between trunk and the sun. Another effective sun screen is an inconspicuous wrapping of burlap around the stem.

Basic pruning guidelines on page 69 also apply to standards, but in addition the accent here is on *symmetry*. After pruning, the head should not have any stems protruding beyond the general outline of the bush.

HOW TO TRAIN CLIMBING ROSES

Climbers whose canes are trained horizontally or are trained upward and arched over will bloom most profusely. Left to its steady upward growth, a long climbing cane will continue to build new tissues to increase only its upward growth. This is a situation known as *apical dominance:* the topmost growth continues at the expense of any lateral growth. When a long, upright cane is arched over or bent down to a horizontal position, however, the apex of growth is thwarted so that many eyes along the cane will begin to grow, each one growing upward. It is these laterals off the main canes and long branches that give you flowers.

If you have a high fence, wall, or side of a house to cover, let the vertical canes grow to about 10 feet long. Then lean them out at an angle from the plant's base on both sides of the plant. Tie canes horizontally and space them 18 to 24 inches apart, paralleling one above the other. Arch the end of each cane downward and tie it in place. Flowering shoots will come from all along the canes. Leave as many canes as you need to achieve the desired height.

Climbers trained horizontally along a low fence or wall will tend to produce flowering shoots from most eyes in the horizontal portions of the canes. Even with horizontal canes, if you arch over about the last 12 inches (after canes have reached the desired length), bloom production will be increased.

JUST-PRUNED CLIMBER shows flowering laterals cut back close to canes, illustrates horizontal training for best bloom.

THE HEALTHY PLANT

Probably more potential rose enthusiasts have had their ardor dampened by long lists of pests and their control measures than by any other aspect of rose culture. Too often the rose has been made to appear the tender, desirable princess constantly endangered by the twin dragons of insects and disease. In truth, roses *are* attractive to various insects and some diseases—but before you read about all the dire possibilities and their controls, let's examine some basic points of plant health.

Your first line of defense against any pests in roses (or, for that matter, in any garden plant) is in the health of the plant itself. Constant spraying won't make a healthy rose out of one that is sickly because of unfavorable climate, wrong exposure, impoverished soil, insufficient water, or lack of nutrients. The sole purpose of sprays and dusts is control of insects and disease.

Much of the formidable-sounding advice on pest control that has reached the rose growing public was aimed toward rosarians who also were avid exhibitors at rose shows. To be in the running for show awards, a rose should be completely unblemished; but for the hundreds of thousands of rose growers who enjoy their roses at home, an imperfect or chewed leaf here and there is not going to dim the roses' beauty nor the gardener's enjoyment of them. Instead of trying for a totally antiseptic garden, try instead for a *balance* between plants and their pests.

Yearly Spray Regime

Every year, your first effort toward establishing basic garden health should be a good spring cleaning (although in mild regions you'll do it in winter). Right after you prune your roses, clean up all leaves and other debris on the ground beneath the bushes, and before new growth shows give both plants and soil a thorough dormant spray—either oil or lime sulfur (calcium polysulfide). These do an excellent job of killing insect eggs and disease spores, which can overwinter on soil, old leaves, or the rose canes themselves, becoming a source of early infestation.

Soon after new growth is out, the first aphid population of the year inevitably arrives. To forestall this first offensive many rose growers use one of the systemic insecticides to eliminate aphids and other sucking insects for about a month.

As the season progresses, when to spray will be a result of observation; and since you will be out enjoying your roses almost daily, early detection of other insects or disease will be easy. Gradually you will evolve your own spray routine to handle whatever insects or diseases invade your area. Remember the following points and you can keep your spraying at a minimum:
• Insects and diseases come in cycles according to the season but collectively are most rampant during the warmest part of the year. So summer will require the most frequent attention to spraying or dusting.
• For either insects or disease, one spray can't be counted upon to achieve control. A follow-up application a week to 10 days later will control newly hatched eggs or spores that your first spray did not reach.
• Many insecticides and fungicides can be combined in one spray solution; you can buy spray concentrates that contain materials to control all principal rose pests. In addition, some foliar fertilizers are compatible with the majority of usual pest control sprays. (But don't assume that all sprays and fertilizers are compatible. See page 27.)
• Fertilizers are only half the story of a healthy plant. The other half is a bushful of healthy foliage that manufactures additional nutrients for the plant (see page 68.) Keep this in mind and you'll regard the spray routine as an indirect tonic for the plants—not solely as a defense effort.

For your more routine pest control operations you have a choice of spraying or dusting. Neither approach is categorically better than the other; the one you choose depends upon personal preference, climatic conditions, how many roses you may have to cover—and, ultimately, on how well it works for you.

Dusting, the older form of control, is in one respect easier: you do no mixing—just put the dust from its package into an applicator and go to work. And when you're finished, there's no need to clean out the duster. This simplicity makes dusting an easy project to do before or after work during the week. Coverage by dusts generally is not quite as thorough as coverage by sprays which can coat each leaf with a film of liquid. Although some people object to the appearance of dust residue on leaves, this residue tends to make dusts a little longer lasting (providing it does not rain) than sprays. In areas where air pollution is frequent, dusts further hamper the leaves' ability to transpire; sprays, with their washing action, are preferable there.

Although duster designs vary (as do the principles by which they work), they all fall into one of two categories—continuous flow or intermittent. The continuous flow sorts are the best (and the least tiring) to use on large or medium sized plantings. For the modest rose garden or just a few plants, one of the intermittent action types, bellows or plunger operated, will do the job nicely, allowing you a little better control of coverage since you determine when the duster will emit its powder. Such dusters also are excellent for small touch-up applications. In fact, you can keep one loaded and ready to go at a moment's notice. Any duster should have a deflecting nozzle so that you can reach the leaves' undersides easily.

Do your dusting when the air is still, for even the slightest breeze tends to blow the dust everywhere but on the roses. Early mornings and evenings usually are the best time to dust. Don't leave your roses looking as if you had dumped sacks of flour on them. A light, relatively inconspicuous coating is enough.

Spraying has several points in its favor. Perhaps most important are the wider variety of materials available for you to use. In addition to water, contact sprays, and briefly residual ones, you also have at your disposal systemic insecticides and fungicides. And with a really fine spray mist, you can penetrate more deeply than dusts do into the cracks and crevices of leaves and flowers. What sprayer you choose will be determined largely by the number of bushes you have. With 100 bushes and a 1-gallon sprayer you'd spend almost as much time filling the sprayer as you'll spend on spraying the bushes. You're much more likely to spray as often as conditions call for if you can make one solution and finish the garden with it. No matter what type you choose, however, it should be designed for easy coverage of the undersides of leaves.

Least expensive and simplest to prepare is the hose-attachment sprayer, a bottle and siphon arrangement that you attach as a nozzle to a garden hose which operates it by water pressure. You measure liquid spray concentrate into the bottle and dilute it with water according to instructions on the spray label. This solution is metered through a needle valve into the hose stream, where it is diluted to the proper concentration as it is discharged through a nozzle on the bottle cap. A bottle that holds enough concentrated solution to make two gallons of spray will cover 10-15 large bushes before you will need to refill it; a six-gallon capacity will spray 40-50 bushes. Unless you clean the siphon part after each spraying, its efficiency may be impaired by a buildup of spray residue—resulting in an improper dilution and poor performance. For the person with not a great number of roses to care for, this type of sprayer may be satisfactory. However, with one it is difficult to cover the undersides of leaves (especially those low on the plant), and it will not put forth as fine a mist as the two types that follow, so you use more spray material. Because of the necessarily high concentration of spray material, these sprayers usually will not handle the dormant season sprays.

Compressed-air tank sprayers are available in capacities of one to six gallons, so they are suitable for both small and fairly large gardens. With these sprayers, the spray concentrate is measured into the tank and diluted with the required amount of water; the spray concentration is always accurate if you are. Then you close the tank top and pump a plunger to get a high pressure for good coverage. Frequently agitate the tank while you are spraying to keep the solution mixed. The drawbacks of the larger ones are their weight and cumbersomeness when loaded. Unless weight-lifting is another of your hobbies, look for the larger models that are provided with a wheel attachment. For freedom of movement among your roses, be sure to get one with the longest possible hose, at the end of which is some sort of provision for a 90° turn in delivery to the spray head. This allows for easy spraying under the leaves.

If you are a really ambitious rose grower with 200 or more plants to spray, you may find a gasoline or electric powered tank sprayer a necessity. Operating at a maintained hose pressure of over 100 pounds, these tanks can throw a finely atomized spray with great force over a considerable area—actually giving greater coverage with less material than other sprayers deliver. With one of these you could cover about 500 large bushes in two hours without having to make any additional dilutions after your initial mixing. Sizes range from 10 gallons on up; tanks usually are mounted on wheels for easy movement around the garden. To assure the best and safest results, buy only a power sprayer that has a built-in agitator.

How to Spray

As important as choosing the right control materials and an efficient applicator is applying the material so it can do the most good.

Thoroughly cover both sides of the leaves. Begin at the base of each bush and work upward with a side-to-side rolling movement of the spray nozzle. Your objective is to cover the underside of every leaf, for this is the region most attractive to insects and disease. By the time you reach the top of the bushes, most of the upper leaf surfaces will have been covered, too, by the "rain-back" of your spray. If not, a quick spray over the tops should finish the job. Manufactured spreader-stickers, when added to a spray solution, will increase a spray's effectiveness by making it coat the leaves and adhere to them better. Even household detergent added to the spray solution (up to 1/4 teaspoon to a gallon of spray) will help.

Spray early in the morning but after most of the dew has left the plants, or in early evening after the sun's heat has decreased. This avoids the possibility of sunburn on wet leaves. To lessen the chance of leaf burn after spraying, tap or gently shake the bushes to rid them of surplus spray drops. To avoid fostering foliage diseases you want dry foliage by nightfall. In a humid-summer climate, morning spraying is the safest.

Do your spraying on a day following a thorough watering. Damp soil tends to shield the plant against leaf burn.

Whenever you spray and whatever material you use, always keep these five points in mind.

• Carefully read all directions on the spray label before using and follow them exactly. If you have any reason to deviate from instructions, or if you are unsure of what controls will combine safely, always seek advice before experimenting. Check with a nearby Consulting Rosarian (see page 35), your county or state department of agriculture, or the nearest university agricultural extension service.

• If you have several choices of material to do one job, choose the least toxic one for first trial.

• Avoid spraying in hot weather. If you must, though, reduce the spray concentration to minimize danger of leaf burn.

• Be very careful of the drift of your sprays and dusts. Many garden chemicals that are relatively safe around human beings are toxic to wildlife—especially to fish. Cover nearby fishponds and bird baths while you spray, and don't dump excess spray or wash out spray equipment where it could easily get into ponds or streams.

• Thoroughly clean out your sprayer after each job. This will keep your sprayer in best working order and prolong its life.

MAJOR ROSE PESTS

The chart on page 77 lists potential problem causers for roses with suggested control for each. A rose garden bothered by even half of these during the year would be unusual. In fact, there are only six afflictions that are widespread and plentiful enough to deserve special mention, and two of these do not occur nationwide.

Insects

Numerous different insecticides are available for the destruction of just about anything that crawls onto your rose plant to damage it. Many of these, however, are somewhat to very hazardous to other living things. The best policy is to determine what insect (or insects) are bothering your roses, then choose the least toxic possible control for your spray. Remember that there may be natural enemies of many pests that could help you as long as you don't eliminate them, too, from your garden.

Aphids are found nearly everywhere and on a tremendous variety of garden plants. Green, red, brown, or black—they are all soft-bodied, about 1/8-inch long. In very early spring they make their season debut on tender new growth; if they congregate in great numbers and are not eradicated they may deform this growth, generally slowing or stunting development. Fortunately, aphids are the easiest pest to eliminate.

Mites—spider mites, red spider, two-spotted mites—whatever you call them their damage is the same: they cause yellowed, dry-looking leaves, sometimes with silvery white webbing underneath. These are a warm weather pest, and the hotter the temperature the more rapidly they develop from egg to adult and the more eggs they lay. Early control is essential, then, before the population explodes.

Mites do their damage by sucking the cell sap from surface tissues of leaves, causing them to change to a yellow or bronze color; the underside then turns pale brown speckled with white dots and webbing. If the mite invasion remains unchecked, the leaves will drop off, and in time an entire plant may be defoliated.

Although mites are so small you barely can see them on a rose leaf, you can check for them in two simple ways. Hold a piece of white paper beneath a suspected leaf and tap the leaf; any mites will fall onto the paper, where you'll be able to see them as little specks vainly scurrying for cover. Or, if you have a magnifying glass, use this to check the undersides of leaves. Lower leaves usually are the first to be affected.

The simplest way to combat mites is with your garden hose and water. Use a nozzle that will give you a fine spray of water, and thoroughly wash off the undersides of your rose leaves. Done several days in succession, this will disrupt their breeding and hatching cycle—and may eliminate the population. It is important that you do this at least three times—three days in a row or every other day—because you need to get the mites that will hatch from eggs that already were laid when you began this hosing-off program.

Agricultural chemists have developed special formulations for mite eradication. You can either buy these separately or use a general purpose spray that contains both insecticides and fungicides. For a really effective mite cleanup, be sure to spray at least twice or preferably three times, waiting 5 days between sprayings. Thoroughly drench the *undersides* of the leaves: that's where the mites are. The first shot kills adult mites, the second should get new ones hatching from eggs that existed at the time you first sprayed and before they mature and lay additional eggs.

Spider mites rather quickly become immune to any one insecticide. If you repeatedly spray for mites throughout a season, changing miticides after several applications will give better control.

Thrips can be the most discouraging of these three pests because their chief target is flowers. Special favorites of theirs are white, yellow and other light-colored varieties. Small as they are (about 1/20th inch long), their rasping and puncturing of petal surfaces can cause considerable discoloration and disfiguration. Thrips attack buds in their early stages, working among the unfolded petals. In severe cases, buds become deformed and fail to open properly, while the damaged petals turn brown and dry. New growth also may be damaged in the same way.

A light misting of buds and blooms twice a week with a specific thrips insecticide during a heavy infestation usually will give good control.

Diseases

Although blackspot, powdery mildew, and rust comprise the "big three" of rose diseases, most rose growers will have to contend with only a "devilish duo." Mildew is found nationwide, but rust and blackspot territories seldom overlap. Planting your roses so that there will be a chance for air circulation around each plant will help minimize foliage disease problems. Roses growing in a single row along a driveway, for example, often will be healthier (other conditions being equal) than the same ones closely planted in a formal garden.

Blackspot is definitely the most devastating of the foliage diseases. Unchecked, it can defoliate a plant at the height of the growing season. Such bushes fail to make normal growth in that year and are much more susceptible to winter damage because plants fail to mature naturally—they continually try to produce new growth to replace lost foliage.

California and the warm, semi-arid regions of the southwest seldom encounter blackspot. Where summer rainfall is common, you find conditions that favor its spread and development: wet leaves, warmth, and splashing water to spread the infection.

The disease is well named. Black spots with irregular, fringed margins appear on the leaves and sometimes on stems. Around the spots, leaf tissue may turn yellow. With especially susceptible varieties and in severe cases, the entire leaf may yellow and drop off.

Blackspot spores live through the winter in lesions on canes and possibly on old leaves fallen to the ground. In spring they germinate and reach new foliage in splashing water from rain or overhead sprinkling. From these infections develop the characteristic spots that then produce great numbers of fresh spores to extend the infection.

Garden sanitation is your first line of defense against the fungus. Keep a watchful eye during the season. If blackspot develops, spray with one of the controls listed below.

Powdery mildew, in a severe attack, does suggest its name: fallout from a flour mill. This is a fungus found virtually everywhere roses are grown, flourishing during times of high humidity but not rainy weather. It is a gray to white, furry or powdery growth that goes after the growth of leaves, stems, and flower buds. Infected leaves quickly become crumpled and distorted and will remain that way even after you kill the fungus. Damage is possible—but less severe—on mature leaves.

Resistance to it varies from one variety to the next. Most old rambler roses wear a gray veil every year.

In contrast to blackspot which spreads in water, mildew is encouraged by a humid atmosphere but needs dry leaves to establish itself. Foggy coastal areas are ideal for its spread. Overcrowded plantings in damp and shady gardens are liable to more severe attacks than are roses in sunny beds where they have free air circulation through and between plants. Unmulched but well-watered roses will be living in a more humid atmosphere than plants with a mulch over the moist soil.

A number of sprays and dusts will control powdery mildew (see below); some of these also are effective against blackspot.

Rust. While the rest of the country is looking for black spots, Western and Southwestern rosarians are seeing red—or, more precisely, rusty-orange. Rust usually appears first in late spring on leaf undersides. Small orange spots enlarge into thick, powdery masses of orange spores as yellow blotches appear on the leaf surface. Easily shaken loose by air currents and rain, they germinate quickly on damp leaves to set up new colonies of infection. In severe and unchecked cases, rust, like blackspot, can defoliate roses.

Here again, garden sanitation goes far toward reducing the incidence of disease. Especially in most regions where roses never go so dormant as to lose all foliage, it is very important that you remove all old leaves from plants as well as from the ground at pruning time. During the season, any of the materials listed below should give adequate control. In the nearly tropical climates of Florida and Hawaii, roses grow all year, so removal of foliage is not a good idea. Gardeners there must rely entirely on foliage sprays for control.

PEST CONTROLS

Problem	Symptom	Control
Aphids	see text	Cygon, Sevin, Pyrethrum, Malathion, Water
Beetles *	chew holes in leaves and petals	Sevin, Malathion to plant and soil
Caterpillars, Worms	chew leaves, flower buds	Diazinon, Sevin, Thurocide, hand pick
Raspberry Cane Borer	bores into centers of stems	hand pick
Rose Midge	buds, new growth turn black, die	Sevin, Sevin-Malathion combination
Spider Mites	see text	Kelthane, Tedion, Diazinon, Cygon, Dibrom, Water
Thrips	see text	Cygon, Sevin, Malathion, Water
Blackspot	see text	Phaltan, Benlate, Maneb, Captan
Powdery Mildew	see text	Acti-dione P-M, Benlate
Rust	see text	Acti-dione P-M, Phaltan, Zineb

*Japanese beetles are a special problem where prevalent; for control, consult your county department of agriculture or local nurseryman.

WINTER PROTECTION

More winter injury results not from low temperature itself but from sudden, rapid, or frequent temperature fluctuation. Moisture in the canes freezes and expands as it does so; the quick freezes break cell walls inside canes and destroy vital plant tissue. Repeated alternations of freezing, thawing, and re-freezing can ruin exposed canes.

Another prime factor in winter damage is desiccation. Winter winds dry out exposed canes, and if soil is frozen, roots cannot take up water to replace lost moisture. If canes have been damaged at all by cold, the injured cells can't resist water loss. In springtime you find shriveled and blackened canes in place of plump, green wood.

Many shrub and species roses can take whatever a northern winter sends their way, and some hybridizers are determinedly working to combine this hardiness with hybrid tea beauty. But until this marriage takes place, most rose growers in areas where snow falls will have to use some form of protection against the elements in order to enjoy the glories of modern hybrid teas, floribundas, and climbers.

Even among modern roses, the varieties do vary considerably in hardiness. Many older yellows, oranges, and bronze shades are more tender than the average, a legacy from 'Persian Yellow' which brought these colors into hybrid teas. Hybrid perpetuals usually are more cold tolerant than hybrid teas, and so are many of the floribundas.

Generally speaking, though, figure that all bush and climbing roses will withstand temperatures down to 10° above zero unprotected. Most shrub and old garden roses can make it on their own until temperature drops to —10°, and many can take much lower readings.

Tips for Winter Survival

Contrary to what you might expect, one purpose of winter protection is to keep roses cold, not warm. What you want are thoroughly dormant canes at a fairly constant temperature—ideally in the 15°-20° range.

Actually, winter protection begins at planting time, for in areas where cold winters prevail, location and exposure can influence greatly the intensity of cold and amount of temperature fluctuation. Cold air seeks the lowest level, so valley gardens will be colder than those on surrounding hillsides. Low pockets in your garden will be consistently colder than elevated or sloping areas, and roses planted there are in danger of being frozen at the bud union unless well insulated. Plantings sheltered from wind—whether by walls, other shrubbery and trees, or your house—are likely to be warmer than exposed plantings and will suffer less from desiccation. Often winter winds are distinctly colder than still air. In regions normally beyond their hardiness limit, climbing roses may survive winters if planted against a house or garage wall that shelters them from wind and raises, by means of reflected heat, the overall low temperatures.

Your care during the growing season also has a great influence on potential cold tolerance. The healthy plant which grew vigorously and was not defoliated by disease or insects will stand a much better chance than the weakling which just managed to exist through the past year. Furthermore, the matured or ripened plant is not nearly so vulnerable as the one which was still actively growing and blooming when frosts hit. Cells in growing stems and canes have high moisture and low starch contents, making them more susceptible to freezing and cell damage; but matured growth, in contrast, has a much higher percentage of solids in the cells in place of moisture. A combination of withholding nitrogen fertilizers about 6 weeks before expected frosts (page 26) and allowing September blooms to stay on the plants to form seed hips will put your roses in the well-ripened state ready to face several months of cold.

Preparation for Protection

No matter what form of winter protection you decide to use, there are some basic preparations and guidelines to follow. Thoroughly clean up all old leaves and spent flowers from the rose bed and strip away any foliage that remains on canes. Left on, leaves will continue to lose moisture, and they are always a potential source of disease infection for the next year. Under rose cones they may decay and spread this to the canes. Be sure to remove all debris and mulch from around plant bases. Then shortly before you expect the ground to freeze, give your bushes one final deep soaking for the year.

As important as protection can be, do refrain from protecting bushes before they need it. If you mound or use cylinders, wait until you have had at least two hard freezes. Styrofoam cones shouldn't go on until the ground is frozen about two inches deep. Cold frame sides may go up at your convenience, but wait until you expect a 15°-20° temperature before putting on the roof.

For roses protected by mounds or cylinders, you'd be wise to tie canes together with soft twine to minimize their whipping around in winter winds. For the same reason cut back any that are taller than three feet.

Uncovering in Spring

Early springtime weather often is unpredictable. Warm days suddenly turn to freezing ones, then back to warm again any number of times before spring arrives for good. So don't be tempted by the first breath of spring to remove the roses' protection. With cold frames and removable-top rose cones, open the roof or top on warm, sunny days but close it if freezes are predicted. If your styrofoam cones have solid tops, take the entire cone off when soil thaws enough so that cones can be pulled off without breaking the flanges. Replace the cones whenever freezes are predicted.

If you use soil mounds, gradually begin to remove soil when it thaws. Do this carefully to avoid breaking any growth that may have begun under the mound.

WINTER PROTECTION METHODS

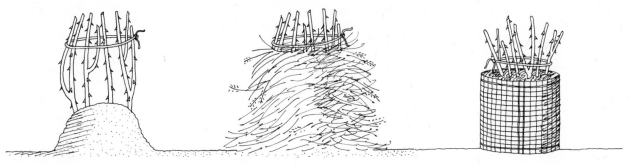

Mound soil at least 12 inches high over bud union of each bush (get soil from another part of garden); cover with straw after mounds freeze to keep mounds frozen.

Cylinder of wire mesh holds soil in place around canes, lets water drain away easily.

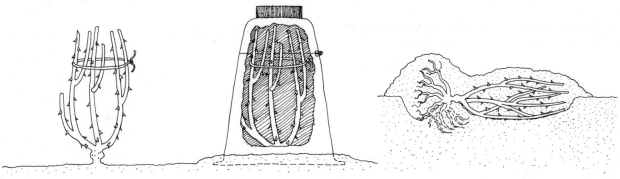

Styrofoam rose cones require tying of canes together, cutting them down to fit cones; brick on top and soil over flanges holds cones in place.

"Minnesota tip" for bush roses: dig roots on one side of bush, bend it over into trench, cover with soil.

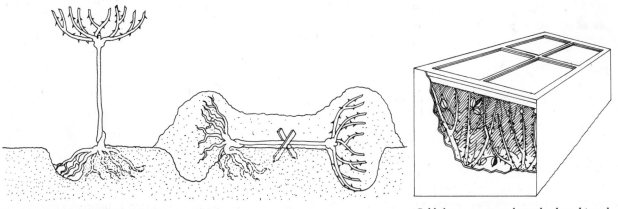

For "tipping" standards, bend plant *over* bud union of roots and trunk, pin trunk to soil, cover.

Cold frame protects large bushes, hinged roof allows ventilation on warm days.

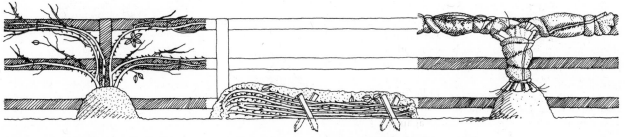

Protect climbers with soil mound where winter is +5°-+15°; cover canes with soil if lows go below −10°; insulate with straw wrapped in burlap for −10°-+5° areas.

Index

boldface numerals indicate illustrations

PHOTOGRAPHERS

William Aplin: 7, 9 (all); **Glenn Christiansen:** cover, 64 (top); **Philip Edinger:** 13 (top); **Gerald R. Fredrick:** 36 (top left), 49 (bottom left); **Alyson Smith Gonsalves:** 13 (bottom), 17, 69; **Lee Klein:** 73; **Ells Marugg:** 4, 24, 27, 29, 36 (top right, bottom left), 37 (all), 39 (all), 42 (all), 44 (all), 45 (top and bottom left, right), 47 (left all, bottom right), 49 (top left, bottom right), 51 (all), 54 (all), 56, 57 (all), 59 (right) 62 (all); **Jack McDowell:** 34, 36 (bottom right), 45 (center left), 47 (top right), 49 (top right), 59 (left all), 64 (bottom right); **John Robinson:** 6; **Darrow M. Watt:** 19 (all).